BLACK REVOLUTIONARY

PRAEGER LIBRARY OF AFRICAN AFFAIRS

This library is intended to provide authoritative and objective studies of the history, politics, economics, and cultures of modern Africa.

The books will fall into three classes:

I. A volume dealing with each African country.
II. Studies of general questions: social, economic, and political affairs, history, and Africa's international relations.
III. Biographies and writings of leading Africans that contribute to an understanding of African development.

The series is under the general editorship of Colin Legum.

CHRISTIANITY AND THE NEW AFRICA *T. A. Beetham*

MAURITANIA *Alfred G. Gerteiny*

ETHIOPIA: A New Political History *Richard D. Greenfield*

ZAMBIA *Richard Hall*

SOUTH AFRICA: A Political and Economic History *Alex Hepple*

BLACK REVOLUTIONARY: George Padmore's Path from Communism to Pan-Africanism *James R. Hooker*

FRENCH-SPEAKING AFRICA SINCE INDEPENDENCE *Guy de Lusignan*

THE CITY IN MODERN AFRICA *Horace Miner* (ed.)

MALAWI: A Political and Economic History *John G. Pike*

NIGERIA *Walter Schwarz*

LESOTHO, BOTSWANA, AND SWAZILAND: The Former High Commission Territories in Southern Africa *Richard P. Stevens*

THE LITERATURE AND THOUGHT OF MODERN AFRICA: A Survey *Claude Wauthier*—Translated by *Shirley Kay*

FORTHCOMING:

RWANDA AND BURUNDI *René Lemarchand*

ANGOLA *Douglas L. Wheeler* and *René Pélissier*

GEORGE PADMORE in 1937 (see p. 46)   (Copyright: Alex Symester)

BLACK REVOLUTIONARY

GEORGE PADMORE'S PATH
FROM COMMUNISM TO
PAN-AFRICANISM

James R. Hooker

PRAEGER PUBLISHERS
New York · Washington · London

PRAEGER PUBLISHERS
111 Fourth Avenue, New York, N.Y. 10003, U.S.A.
5, Cromwell Place, London S.W.7, England

Published in the United States of America in 1967
by Praeger Publishers, Inc.

Second printing, 1970

© 1967 James R. Hooker, London, England

Library of Congress Catalog Card Number: 67–22702

PRINTED IN THE UNITED STATES OF AMERICA

Contents

Acknowledgements

MANY PEOPLE have helped me write this book; a smaller but still impressive number refused to help. It would be unfair to single out especially helpful ones, and even more indiscreet to particularise the obstructionists. It is a temptation which I forego reluctantly, however, especially in the latter case. But for all those who helped, whether in New York or Los Angeles, London or Port of Spain, Paris or Tel Aviv, whether black or brown or white, my very great thanks, and I hope none feels betrayed. To all those in the other camp, may I again express my disappointment that you thought so much of the cold war or of race and so little of George Padmore that you doubted his reputation could withstand my scrutiny.

I wish to express my gratitude to the Director of the African Studies Center at Michigan State University, Dr Charles Hughes, for the funds which supported my researches. For several years he approved expenses on my assurance that something would come from it after all. I hope his investment has been returned.

My debt to those who made private papers available to me is expressed on page 159.

J.R.H.

Abbreviations used in text

AAPO	*All-African Peoples' Organisation*
AFL	*American Federation of Labor*
ANLC	*American Negro Labor Congress*
CIC	*College of the Immaculate Conception (Trinidad)*
CIO	*Congress of Industrial Organisations*
CPP	*Convention Peoples' Party*
CPUSA	*Communist Party of the United States of America*
IAIYL	*International Anti-Imperialist Youth League*
IASB	*International African Service Bureau*
ILD	*International Labor Defense*
ILP	*Independent Labour Party*
ISH	*International of Seamen and Harbour Workers*
ITUC–NW	*International Trades Union Congress of Negro Workers*
KAU	*Kenya African Union*
KPD	*German (Weimar) Communist Party*
Kutvu	*University of the Toilers of the East*
LAI	*League Against Imperialism*
LCP	*League of Coloured Peoples*
MCF	*Movement for Colonial Freedom*
NAACP	*National Association for the Advancement of Colored People*
NASSO	*National Association of Socialist Students' Organisation*
NCCL	*National Council for Civil Liberties*
NCNC	*National Council for Nigeria and the Cameroons*
NNC	*National Negro Congress*
NWA	*Negro Welfare Association*
PAF	*Pan-African Federation*
RILU	*Red International of Labour Unions (Profintern)*
TUUL	*Trade Union Unity League*
UGCC	*United Gold Coast Convention*
WASU	*West African Students' Union*
WANS	*West African National Secretariat*
WFTU	*World Federation of Trade Unions*

I

From Trinidad to New York:
Nurse Becomes Padmore

TO BE A WEST INDIAN is an especially difficult task. It is far easier to stop being one, to escape to London or Halifax or New York, even to Freetown or Accra, there to use those powers and skills which, in the islands, bring so few benefits. If it is true that the Indies have no history, but are merely passive bits of exotic scenery on which various Europeans have performed their selfish exploits, it equally is true that West Indians are bowed under the necessity of remembering these cruel tales. There is no tendency to repress their recollection; rather one senses what amounts to very nearly a preoccupation. The impact of Europeans seems relatively slight in West Africa, where it has been exerted longest; the old slavers' forts and barracoons, when not ignored, usually seem curious, detached from present life, 'interesting'. Elmina would scarcely be used by Ghanaians to explain current short-comings, but, in the islands, the slave master's whip may be heard cracking into flesh on all sides. One hears it in calypso, one reads of it in research libraries which preserve this gruesome heritage, and it crops up in general conversation.

Such matters necessarily present the question of race relations in a simple form; white mastery and black humiliation, a relation-ship which did not change materially when slavery was outlawed. The West Indian of African descent (a phrase much regarded in that quarter today) who emerged from formal slavery might be forgiven if he saw little to commend the new arrangements, for the 'apprenticeship' which followed hard upon the brief period of idle freedom from the cane fields seemed scarcely better. Year by year, decade after decade, the whites still seemed in command and the blacks continued to pursue their traditional lowly jobs. The black man's disdain for the land, his craving for advance, led him to the professions, as the English of an earlier age had defined them. Medicine first, and after that law and teaching claimed his attention. A few went into businesses, which mostly failed, and a few entered the newer professions. One such was George Padmore's father, entomologist without university qualifications, schoolmaster and supervisor of agricultural instruction—a strange man on the double count that science and experimental farming were not the normal interests of aspiring blacks at the turn of the century.

Malcolm Ivan Meredith Nurse, better known as George Padmore, was born in Arouca District, Tacarigua, Trinidad, probably in the year 1902.* His father, a local schoolmaster, James Hubert Alfonso Nurse, who had married Anna Susanna Symister of Antigua, was an accomplished naturalist who, if white, no doubt would have advanced further in government service. As it was, he rose to become senior agricultural instructor in the Department of Education and spent his retirement in writing an exhaustive (and unpublished) geography of the West Indies. His own father, a Barbadian named Alphonso Nurse, had been born a slave; he had become a master mason, migrated to Trinidad and lived for more than a century. Tales of the slave days and 'apprenticeship' were part of the young Malcolm's heritage. On several occasions in later life, he referred to himself as the grandson of a slave. According to one report, James Nurse went so far as to become a Muslim and, in order to eradicate this past of slavery, assigned an Arabic name to his son.

Shortly after his birth, Malcolm was brought to Port of Spain where his father took a position in a city school. Malcolm's closest friends were his cousin Alex Symister, another named Errol Padmore, and a schoolmaster's son, C. L. R. James. Though they

---

* He claimed 1903, which is the date accepted by his in-laws and wife. But the marriage register differs and the birth records long since were consumed by ants and stained by water. Those who have seen the cavalier treatment of Vital Statistics in Port of Spain will agree that the survival of any is surprising.

did their share of kite flying, and once set fire to a carnival dancer's costume, they were in general rather serious boys, especially Nurse. Though he impressed strangers with the imperturbable gaiety of an amused worldling, he had also a reputation for purposeful action. He disliked one of his teachers who tried to limit the boys' views to the island, which stifled Negro progress.

After finishing at the Tranquillity School, he went to St Mary's College of the Immaculate Conception, the secondary school of the Holy Ghost Fathers.[1] Most of his friends attended the other prestige secondary establishment, the Queen's Royal College. Nurse was at the College of the Immaculate Conception (CIC) for two years only, 1914 and 1915, in Standards IIB and IIA. His career was undistinguished; one of the staff who remembers him slightly, Father Leonard Graf, was unable to anticipate greatness. Nurse transferred to the Pamphylian High School, a private institution, from which he graduated in 1918. There is some confusion here, as the diploma from the high school, which Nurse submitted to the registrar at Fisk University, certified that he had attended that school from January 1913 to December 1917.[2] Of course, his two years at CIC may have been incorporated without mention by the Pamphylian authorities. In any case, Nurse passed out satisfactorily in the usual Cambridge Certificate subjects—Geometry, Latin, Greek, French, History, Algebra and English Literature—as well as in those such as Tropical Entomology and Agricultural Science which were of more local significance. He also concurrently attained first place on the honours list in the preliminary examination of the Medical Board of Trinidad in June 1916, and in August was pronounced qualified to become a student in pharmacy.[3]

Shortly after graduation he took a job with the Trinidad Publishing Company, reporting shipping news for the now defunct *Weekly Guardian*. His friend and brother-in-law, Baden Semper, recalls that Malcolm was a poor reporter. The job bored him, there was no scope for thoughtful writing and he detested his editor, Edward J. Partridge, an Englishman who demanded subservience from his black staff. When Partridge died, Nurse wrote that he had been 'one of the most arrogant agents of British Imperialism I have ever encountered. I held him in utter contempt, and had hoped to use my pen in exposing his role before the colonial workers and peasants whom he oppressed through his

3

dirty sheet the *Guardian*.' Nurse would not defer, his work was termed unsatisfactory, and finally there was an indignant exchange and he was fired.

Unfortunately, he had responsibilities, for in the meantime he had married Julia Semper, daughter of Constabulary Sergeant-Major George Semper, a neighbour. While living in Norfolk Street, Nurse had met the Semper girls, Iris and Julia, and had helped them with their work for the Coterie of Social Workers, a bluestocking assembly which published the *Coterie Clarion*. He had grown to admire their father, the first black man to reach the rank of senior non-commissioned officer. After a rather lengthy courtship, the couple were married at All Saints (Anglican) Church in Queen's Park West on Wednesday, September 10, 1924, by Father Arthur Humbersley. The wedding was followed by a reception at the police barracks in Belmont Circular Road (beneath today's towering Hilton Hotel). Nurse and his bride were resplendent, she in a lengthy train, he in tails. Their best man, Errol Padmore, recently back from Venezuela, commemorated the event in lengthy and not altogether unpoetic verse.

Since leaving secondary school, Nurse had dreamed of higher education. Opportunities for study in the colony were negligible and little or no assistance was given to able scholars for travel abroad. Professional training usually meant residence in the United Kingdom, which very few achieved. Those who did often made their mark—for instance, the barrister Henry Sylvester Williams, one of the originators of the Pan-African movement—but their number was stable and small. England was not the only home of universities and professional schools, of course; one could always consider the United States. Naturally, in a British possession, there was much objection to this course, for American credentials were suspect. Indeed, American dental schools alone were regarded as worthy of Trinidad accreditation. Nevertheless, from a fairly early time, Nurse seems to have desired an American medical training. In September 1924, his name having been reached on the United States immigration quota, his chance had come, and he sailed for Fisk University in Nashville, Tennessee. His wife, by then pregnant, remained in Trinidad to bear their first and only child. Some measure of Nurse's racial pride is apparent from his instruction that the baby, regardless of sex,

4

must be named Blyden. In June 1925, Julia dutifully named their daughter after the man who was, as Nurse thought, the greatest West Indian.[4]

Nurse proposed to study medicine, and to this end proffered letters of recommendation from the Acting Assistant Inspector of Schools, the Pharmaceutical Society of Trinidad and a member of the island's medical board. He landed at Ellis Island from the ship *Mayaro* on December 29, 1924, being designated an 'African Black' by the immigration service, and announced his destination as Nashville, Tennessee. However this may be, he did not enrol at Fisk until the fall term, 1925, in the meantime taking a course in sociology at Columbia University, which in June of that year recorded his address as 124 West 135th Street, Manhattan. By the time he arrived at Fisk, Nurse had decided already against the study of medicine, and he shifted to law, in preparation for which he began reading political science. He also retained his journalistic connections by joining the student newspaper, the *Fisk Herald*. Nurse was an exceptionally able speaker, much in demand when colonial issues were aired. In 1926, he was one of seventy-five state-wide delegates to a conference on 'religion and the world', sponsored by the Student Volunteer Movement, at which he appeared on the platform alongside such celebrities as Dr Mordecai Johnson, the President of Howard University. In April 1927, apropos of another conference, one of the organisers wrote: 'Mr Nurse is by all means one of the outstanding students in Nashville today. I have heard him speak several times and his service is in great demand among the white colleges of Nashville. Recently, in a meeting at Vanderbilt University, he and two Scarritt College Professors were the principal speakers on the present situation in China. . . . So strongly do I feel that we should have him, that I am willing to say that even if we did not get any other foreign student in my area, I should by all means desire Nurse to be a representative.'[5] 'He was well-liked on the campus and carried himself in a dignified manner, always well groomed', the assistant registrar recalls.[6]

The atmosphere at Fisk in the 1920s was troubled. At the time of Nurse's arrival, President Fayette McKenzie had restricted student activities, the Ku Klux Klan had expressed concern about agitators, communists and 'new Negroes', and a few months earlier nearly three-quarters of the students had gone on strike (thereby earning the approval of Dr W. E. B. DuBois).[7] For whatever reason, and his wife has hinted at Klan threats, Nurse did not take a Fisk degree. Instead, he decided to enter one of the New York City universities. In 1926, his wife also arrived in New York, leaving their baby at home with its grandparents. He left Fisk with a first-rate record; his transcript showed he did especially well in International Relations, Negro Sociology, Botany and Zoology. While at Fisk, Nurse established contact with Benjamin Azikiwe, whom he met next year at Howard University. In March 1927 Nurse asked Azikiwe to help him establish an African student organisation 'to foster racial consciousness and a spirit of national-ism aiming at the protection of the sovereignty of Liberia'. This is one of the earliest examples of his Liberian preoccupation.[8]

Perhaps because of his own Roman Catholic education, Nurse first thought of entering Fordham Law School. But the fees were too high, and so in September 1927 he matriculated at the Law School of New York University. He never attended classes or took examinations, and was dropped in December. Meanwhile, he had enrolled at the Law School of Howard University, presumably because the Communist Party, which he joined shortly after reaching the Greenwich Village campus, wanted him to do so. Howard had at that time the largest contingent of foreign students in the country: 200, of whom 150 were from British dependencies. He was under party discipline from mid-1927, and, by 1928 at the latest, adopted the cover name George Padmore when engaged in party business. This was compounded of his friend's surname and his father-in-law's first name. As he somewhat ingenuously wrote to his friend Dudley Cobham, a Port of Spain docker, now an alderman of that city and a stalwart supporter of Dr Eric Williams's government: 'You see, all revolutionaries are compelled to adopt false names to hide their identity from the Government.'

That he led this double life quite successfully is attested by Dr Ralph Bunche, one of his instructors at Howard, who knew Nurse quite well and was unaware of the party connection. Nurse/ Padmore's best publicised act was a protest which he organised on the occasion of Sir Esme Howard's visit to the campus. The then British Ambassador to the United States was invited to dedicate the university's International House at 2447 Georgia Avenue and

Padmore objected. Together with another West Indian, a medical student named Cyril C. Ollivierre (today an eye specialist in New York), he circulated* lengthy mimeographed documents from an organisation called the International Anti-Imperialistic Youth League. Padmore seemed to be its secretary. Sir Esme was attacked not only as the representative of history's most bloated empire, but also for his alleged role in procuring the deportation of Marcus Garvey from the United States to his native Jamaica—Ollivierre was president of the campus Garvey Club.[9] President Johnson apologised for this embarrassing incident, which, he explained, was the act of an outsider, for there was no George Padmore enrolled at Howard. As Ollivierre remembers it, Johnson was sympathetic to the students' aims, but it is possible that he did not know that Nurse and Padmore were one.

Nurse rapidly became as well known at Howard as he had been in Nashville. Bunche recalls a speech Nurse 'made one noon in the centre of the campus, in which he denounced just about everybody and everything connected with the university, in fluent, ringing rhetoric'. And the reporter who covered the mock presidential election of 1928 for the student paper, *The Hilltop*, wrote that Nurse's presentation of the Communist Party's case, so far as it touched upon race matters, was 'probably the most effective feature during this election'. He was 'bright and industrious', according to another of his professors, Dr Metz Lochard, later of the *Chicago Defender*. In Lochard's opinion, Nurse had 'much more drive than most American Negroes' because he was a product of the 'British system which did not completely silence their grievances at home'. 'He was admired immensely by both faculty and student body. He spoke at the chapel many times. He was our favourite speaker.' To his sister-in-law Iris, Nurse confided that, in his four years in the United States, he had 'covered much ground and achieved quite a record both as a student and a leader of youth'. Indeed, along with a fellow Trinidadian, Eugene Corbie,

* Another account of this incident has Padmore flinging the papers in Sir Esme's face, an act inconsistent with his character as well as an inefficient distribution procedure. Ollivierre, who was the connection between Azikiwe and Padmore/Nurse, got the former a job with Professor Alain Locke. Zik spent a year at Howard, during which Padmore was an important campus figure. See Jones-Quartey, *A Life of Azikiwe*, pp. 78 and 246.

who died shortly after a brilliant career at the City College of New York, he was, he reckoned, one of the 'two most outstanding coloured youth leaders in college circles in the country . . .'. He was a rather priggish youth, to judge from his correspondence, quite keen on winning his way in the world. American racism bore down on him, but at the same time the 'new Negro' reaction impressed the young West Indian. 'I should like to see a little more of that spirit develop in Trinidad', he wrote to his wife's sister. Though never reconciled to American conduct—'Life, habits, customs and institutions of this country are entirely different to ours and never appeal to one who has had a decent British training' —he had succeeded in that strange land; indeed he was 'now on the threshold of a great career'. 'I have always succeeded in all my undertakings', he informed Iris, 'and I feel that with God's help I shall get through to the end as successfully as I have begun.' Perhaps rather odd sentiments for a leading Negro member of the Communist Party, but understandable. He was, in short, poor but buoyant as the 1920s closed in America.

An anecdote suggests his power of persuasion. Ollivierre and Padmore met as dishwashers at Camp Kinderland, a resort for leftwing working-class Jewish New Yorkers which had opened in 1923 in Hopewell Junction. When washing up for a large party, the two fell far behind. As the stacks of dirty dishes mounted in the steaming kitchen and the waiters' voices became more and more abusive, Nurse grew indignant. Ollivierre, a more pliant man, commenced to scant his efforts, merely dipping plates for a cursory swish, a course of action which brought about his downfall but in the meantime earned him a respite. Nurse refused to do so. Instead, he stopped, rolled down his sleeves (always one for proper dress) and marched to the dining room where he excoriated the startled diners for abetting the exploitation going on beneath their noses. Some of the men marched back through the swinging doors and helped catch up under Nurse's supervision.

During this period, he travelled extensively for the Communist Party. By 1928, he was important enough to begin to appear in the New York *Daily Worker*, and, with Richard B. Moore, began editing a party paper in Harlem, the *Negro Champion* (which became the weekly *Liberator* late in 1929). He was involved in the Harlem Workers' Center and attended Bertram Wolfe's Workers'

School downtown at party headquarters. To earn a living, Nurse worked on the Hudson River Line boats and was a janitor in the Times Building. According to Ollivierre, on several occasions his friend augmented his limited but superior wardrobe with cast-offs from office wastepaper-baskets. Nurse drove constantly between Washington and New York, and all in all provided an excellent example of the astonishing vigour and singleness of purpose one associates with the determined party activist. There is no reason to doubt that he did all this because the communists alone seemed to offer an answer to the colour question: to them, it did not exist. If in retrospect it appears that even they saw the Negro as a subsidiary problem, this certainly was not clear in the late 1920s.

Yet even then one could discern in Nurse's behaviour what the Communist Party later identified as the tendency towards racism. According to Ollivierre, when the Communist Party would not back Nurse's views, he would persuade the Negro press to attack the party. This often brought the downtown theoreticians to heel. Nurse was, in short, a black chauvinist. But he argued that chauvinism in a black man, as the world was structured, was simply the quest for equality. He also, somewhat contradictorily, tried quite hard, in the face of most available evidence, to insist that the freedom of the working class could be effected only through inter-racial unity. The new leftwing trade unions were his greatest hope.[10] He was not the principal organiser of such bodies, as some of his few Ghanaian admirers later alleged, but in association with Moore, who was national organiser for the party's principal organ in this field, the American Negro Labor Congress (ANLC), he did travel and speak constantly. The fact remained that the strike at the Gastonia, North Carolina, textile mills[11] offered the only proof that this policy could work. There, Fred Beals of the National Textile Workers' Union had insisted upon organising both black and white, with initial success. But, as Nurse wrote, the distance between black and white workers in the American South was as great as that between Jews and Russian peasants under the czarist dispensation.

Thus far, Padmore seems to have paid Africa little attention. The assumption current in Communist Party circles was that Negro Americans would provide the vanguard, in the absence of

9

capable Africans. In the ignorant dicta of J. W. Ford, one of the party's black functionaries: 'In spite of the denial of opportunity to the Negro under American capitalism, his advantages are so far superior to those of the subject colonial Negroes in the educational, political and industrial fields that he is alone able to furnish the agitational and organizational ability that the situation demands.'[12] (A generation later the reverse came to be assumed: a strong Africa seemed necessary for Negro America's freedom. The transition is an interesting piece of intellectual history. Even in his time Ford ignored the outstanding success of West Indians and Africans in Negro institutions.) Unfortunately for Ford's thesis, most Negroes did not join the Communist Party, and those who did, such as Ford himself, were careerists, or lacked ability and skill, such as the occasional tenant farmer or mill-hand who was induced to appear on party occasions. This partly explains Padmore's success, though it does not belittle his astounding ascent. No doubt it was a relief to William Z. Foster and other party executives to gain so selfless a worker. The other sort was all too common.*

At the Fourth Congress of the Profintern—or Red International of Labour Unions (RILU)—in March 1928, delegates, perhaps because it was the first with genuine African participants, called for an intensification of activity in that continent, and instructed 'the Executive Bureau to call together the representatives of the Negro workers for the purpose of working out immediate practical measures for carrying into effect the policy laid down in regard to the question of organizing Negro workers in the United States and in Africa'.[13] This was clear, but not new; as far back as 1923, the RILU had resolved that Task No. 7 was: 'A struggle against exploitation and enslavement of the working masses in the colonies, without distinction of race.'[14] This was amplified and confused in the programme of the ANLC (c. 1926) which spoke of: 'Millions of Negroes in Africa, Central America and the West Indies [who] suffer under imperialist aggression and domination. . . . Robbed

---

* Benjamin Gitlow, one of the CPUSA founders, speaking of Ford, later wrote in *I Confess*, pages 454–5: 'Ignorant of trade union matters, representing no Negro workers, and even more ignorant of the Communist movement, he had an innate shrewdness and ability to take advantage of situations that had to do with his own advancement.'

of their lands, their village communes deliberately destroyed, the once independent and happy peasantry of Africa and Asia is being forced into the mines and privately-owned plantations of white imperialists.'

Now, however, bombast and imprecision were succeeded by action. The first stage was the formation of a front. Guided by a German member of the Comintern, Willi Münzenberg, a remarkable collector of respectable signatures, a very successful conference was held in Brussels (February 10–15, 1927) to co-ordinate anti-colonial measures and to reconcile the differences between the antipathetic Amsterdam (or Second) and Red (or Moscow) international labour union bodies. Persons of great eminence—among them Professor Albert Einstein and the novelist Henri Barbusse—attended. All told, representatives from thirty-four countries in five continents were convened, partly at the expense of International Labor Defense, yet another of the Moscow organs. The result was the formation of a League Against Imperialism and for National Independence (usually styled LAI).[15] The presidency was vested in the hands of the dynamic and capable Fenner Brockway, the militantly pacifist official of the British Independent Labour Party. Despite Brockway's subsequent resignation at the urging of his Second International superiors, the LAI remained a valuable Communist International (Comintern) property until the line changed in 1935.

The lengthy (July 15 to September 1, 1928) Sixth Congress of the Comintern considered this background of recent revolutionary planning and approved a programme designed by Stalin, who now controlled both party and state and hence the overseas parties as well. His spokesman, the Finnish academic, Professor Otto Kuusinen—who, Padmore later wrote, had never seen more than a dozen black people prior to the Congress—demanded approval of the 'black republic' thesis, the notion that in South Africa and certain portions of the American South the blacks should be considered nationalities, not racial minorities or majorities without power, and that, consequently, separate areas should be established for their home rule. One sees and can sympathise with the view that 'any definition of the Negro Question which would take race prejudice as its point of departure or as its very essence, would lead into a maze of blind alleys, or into either outright segregation or white chauvinism. . . . What then is the nature of the Negro Question? . . . Historical, economic and social data substantiate the Communist view that the problem of the Negro is the problem of an oppressed nation.'[16] But, in 1928, this was sacrificing a great deal to theory. Both in South Africa and in America, the parties foundered on racist realities.

Padmore, who was campaigning for the party's presidential candidate, William Z. Foster, thought the Kuusinen proposal a 'fantastic scheme' designed to capture sections of the disintegrating Garvey organisation, that 'peculiar form of Negro Zionism which . . . toys with the aristocratic attributes of a non-existent "Negro Kingdom". . . .'* All his speeches reported in the *Daily Worker* that election year suggest that he saw the party as an instrument to aid the black man in America, not set him apart from it. His last years—when he gave up on the West Indies, displayed little interest in America, and indeed narrowed his vision till he saw Africa alone—were in antithesis to his youthful mode. True, he did talk somewhat mysteriously of moving to Liberia after graduation from Howard Law School. 'Perhaps you would like to go out to Liberia with us', he asked Iris Semper. 'We plan to live there but that is after a visit home for Blyden.' As we shall see, it was Liberia in a sense which precipitated his break with Moscow, and it was Liberia which hastened his death.

Padmore did not figure in the Sixth Congress, despite the assertions of some scholars,[17] but in the next year he was sent, along with James W. Ford, to the Second Congress of the LAI, which met near the zoological gardens in Frankfurt from July 20 to 31.[18] Ford did the talking, as usual attacking reformism, Second

---

* Dedicated comrades in South Africa felt the same way. As in America, members of the South African Communist Party were expelled for criticising the black republic scheme. This party was controlled from London and the British Communist Party, which if anything became more slavishly Stalinist than the United States Communist Party, accused their colonial comrades of opportunism and rejoiced that since accepting the Kuusinen line 'the CP of South Africa has developed from a small party of about 250 whites to a membership of nearly 2,000 natives'. The Comintern, they were told, 'is considering the formation of a mass black party in South Africa'. Of such pathetic stuff were their successes made. (Nyasaland Archives, GOB/G85, 22/4/30, a report from the police agent within the London District Committee concerning a CP meeting, April 12, 1930.)

International chauvinism, the South African National Congress, Garveyism, naïve members of the West African Students' Union (WASU) in London, and labour 'mis-leaders' such as Clements Kadalie in South Africa and A. Philip Randolph in the United States.

The Congress was disappointing to the Comintern. In January the LAI General Council (securely in Comintern hands) had met in Cologne, demanding an end to the customary reliance upon national bourgeoisies in backward areas. But the delegates at Frankfurt ignored this injunction. Reformists dominated the proceedings. Indeed, William Pickens of the National Association for the Advancement of Coloured People (NAACP) actually argued against immediate European evacuation of Africa and attacked the Negro nationality line. Of the 200 delegates, only 84 could be considered colonials, and of this number only 15 came directly to the Congress from colonies. Garan Kouyaté was the sole African representative present and only 20 trade unionists and 3 peasants participated. Ford called for the formation of black trade unions, which would seem to contradict the party line, though delegates did not say so. In the event, Negro delegates were instructed to organise a Negro workers' conference in 1930. Padmore wrote to Cobham: 'I was elected a member of the organisational committee and assigned to get together the names of all West Indian labour organisations.' Cobham was asked to help compile the list.* Padmore also remarked to Cobham that the year had been a good one academically, 'despite the fact that I am always kept busy writing articles for the American and European revolutionary press'.

The Frankfurt Congress marked Padmore's entry into the sphere of international communist activity and signalled the end of his American period. Though he was a delegate to the Trade Union Unity League (TUUL) convention in Cleveland immediately after the conclusion of the LAI meeting, and spoke vigorously against white chauvinism and black Uncle Tomism, it was his final contribution to the American party's efforts in the field of Negro labour.[19]

The Cleveland convention was ignored outside party circles;

* Padmore normally mailed copies of communist literature to Cobham concealed in copies of the London *Times* and other trustworthy organs. Dockers naturally were a principal target.

inside, it was considered important enough to warrant a verbal
report to Moscow. And this time Foster decided to take Padmore
with him, an indication that the young Trinidadian had arrived
at the 'threshold of a great career'. Whether Padmore knew that
Foster and the Comintern expected him to stay in the Soviet Union
is debatable, for he had told Cobham that he would be back at
Howard on October 15 to finish his last year. Nevertheless, the
eloquent young man was given two one-way tickets. Only then did
his wife learn of the Moscow move. He apparently tested her without mentioning that she was included in the venture (it was her
understanding, she told me in 1965, that he was going alone—a
course which in any case she deprecated; presumably he never told
her of the other ticket because of this). They often had quarrelled
about his political activities ('New York University was my
undoing', as she said); this time she refused to condone them: if
he went, he went alone. During this domestic unpleasantness,
Padmore's pocket was picked and both tickets, plus what money he
had, disappeared. He 'borrowed' a coat and hat from Ollivierre,
and with three dollars subscribed by friends, sailed for Russia.
As he was a quota entrant to the United States and was going to
unrecognised Communist Russia, Padmore was refused a re-entry
permit. Years later he admitted this had been a foolish mistake,
according to his wife.*

Five days before Christmas 1929, Foster and Padmore delivered
their report and commentary. According to the *Daily Worker*,
Padmore stressed the significance of the Cleveland affair and once
again trotted out the Gastonia textile strike as evidence of the
dramatic shift in American trade union racial policies. He impressed Alexander Losovsky and Dmitri Zakarevich Manuilsky,
quickly became an important official in the Profintern, and during
1930 lectured on colonialism at Kutvu (the University of the
Toilers of the East), a training centre for colonial students.†

* The *mea culpa* letter, which he sent her in 1934, disappeared, Mrs
Nurse told me, in a general house-cleaning she undertook in 1963.

† Apart from the state universities and institutes, there were four
centres of advanced education run by the party: the Lenin University
which catered to students from the West; the Sun Yat Sen University
which served the Chinese; Kutvu for those from the rest of Asia and
from Africa; and the Academy of Red Professors, which trained faculty
for the others and for party work. In *Pan-Africanism or Communism?*,

Whether he collaborated with Stalin, as the Negro American press occasionally asserted at a later date,[20] is doubtful, but he did move in important circles, first as an American specialist,[21] then as head of the RILU's Negro Bureau. The Fourth Congress of the RILU had the United States and South Africa principally in mind when it established this department, but some indication of Padmore's responsibilities appears from an obituary which he wrote years after he left the movement.[22] He contributed articles on Negro and African matters to the English-language *Moscow Daily News*, then edited by the man held responsible for Stalin's failure with Chiang Kai-shek, Michael Borodin (or Guesenberg). Losovsky put Padmore on the commission which investigated the ultra-left deviationist charges levelled at Li Li-san by Mao Tse-tung. 'Li Li-sanism' was the doctrine which called for the Chinese revolution to be led by the urban proletariat, as the rural masses were inert. Padmore agreed with the commission that the accused was 'fundamentally a young romantic adventurer'. The two were of an age. The Negro American journalist, Homer Smith (alias Chatwood Hall), who knew him slightly in this period, thought of Padmore as a top person, one who pulled strings and did not move among lesser fry.[23]

This was a time of great personal power, which must be remembered when considering Padmore's succeeding years of penury and political impotence. Those who accused him of relishing influence, of revelling in power during his final, Ghanaian, period, for the most part did not know that he once had access to even greater authority. Living as he did at the dizzy height allowed important foreign comrades, supervising the activities of the world's black peoples, he experienced none of the misery which the Russian people knew intimately. Many years later he told of his shock when a young woman he had invited to share a meal with him in his Moscow flat asked if she might take the table scraps to her family.

In after years, he told two stories which illustrated that throughout he maintained a certain reserve, a certain scepticism about his qualifications for such treatment. On one May Day he was given a place on the reviewing stand in Red Square, and noticed

page 318, Padmore wrote that, in his time, 'there were never more than a dozen Africans at Kutvu'.

with amusement the puzzled glances cast his way by foreign observers. He also claimed a brief career with the Moscow City Soviet, to which he was elected, along with Kaganovitch and Stalin. He consented under protest to stand for election. He spoke no Russian (he had no facility with languages), he was terribly busy, he would feel a fool. Manuilsky, who had approached him, guaranteed that neither expertise in the tongue nor free time counted. Padmore's first and only task as a member of this body came when he was introduced to a group of British visitors, who were reminded that men of Padmore's colour were unlikely to rise so high in Trinidad.

From time to time he 'came out': occasionally carrying funds for overseas parties (one story involves a small café near Euston Station, London, where he met Harry Pollitt of the British Communist Party, another hints at secret visits to South Africa and Congo, a third mentions an interrogation by the police in Dakar, of which he later wrote: 'I know Dakar and environs quite well . . .'[24]); often performing wryly amusing tasks for the party giants ('British razor blades for Molotov', he later put it); on several occasions recruiting young colonials such as Johnstone Kamau (alias Jomo Kenyatta)* to Moscow, and on one trip in 1932 failing to enlist his old childhood friend, C. L. R. James, then resident in London. Padmore was still in his twenties, he was successful at a task for which he was well equipped and he was committed to a vital cause. The mediocre scholar, the man too big for Trinidad, had come far from Tacarigua. He never returned to America, the law, or the respectable world of Negro professionalism. After March 1930, when he notified Howard University officials of his withdrawal, he never looked back.

* With unsatisfactory results, for Kenyatta became rather stridently anti-communist, at least among friends, something the British authorities in Kenya never knew. (See the Corfield Report.)

2

Top Negro Descending: Padmore Becomes an Unperson

THE FIRST INTERNATIONAL conference of Negro workers, which Padmore had helped plan, was held in Hamburg from July 7 to 9, 1930. The idea for this meeting had come out of the Second Congress of the LAI the previous summer, when the provisional committee, chaired by J. W. Ford of the TUUL, had recommended meeting in London, the centre of imperial power. The Labour government of Ramsay MacDonald soon refused them venue, which was no surprise to those familiar with Parliamentary Labour Party reformism and trade union views concerning colonies. The shift to Hamburg was indicative of the good relations the communists had with the administration of that city, where, among other things, some of the police were party members. Most colonials were denied passports, but even so seventeen delegates met: a number of Americans (including a woman textile worker), a white man representing the black workers of South Africa, and workers from Jamaica, Trinidad, Nigeria, Gambia, Sierra Leone, Gold Coast and the Cameroons. The Jamaican came as a Garveyite, but was converted. French, Belgian and Portuguese Africa and the British East African territories were not represented.*

Padmore asserted that Negro struggles were connected with the revolutionary movements in Asia. Both demonstrated the growing awareness of coloured peoples that they could control their own

* A good example of the exaggerations which litter accounts of Padmore's life is Roi Ottley's statement (in *No Green Pastures*, part of which was based upon Padmore interviews) that 1,000 attended this conference.

destinies. He warned against existing Negro leadership and the pitfalls of 'Garveyism, Pan-Africanism [an interesting touch, this, when his later life is considered], national reformism and trade union reformism', and he worried about the Negro American tendency to analyse African problems in an American light. Frank Macauley of the Nigerian National Democratic Party (who died the following year) exhorted black men to look at the feverish war preparations going forward and remember the thankless sacrifices blacks had made during the 1914–18 War. At the end of the conference a new international commission was appointed. J. W. Ford, Israel Hawkins and Padmore were to represent the American workers, G. Reid stood for the West Indies, Frank Macauley for Nigeria, G. Small for Gambia and Albert Nzula represented South Africa. Haiti, Liberia and East Africa were to be represented later, and Garan Kouyaté of Soudan (now Mali) was to stand for French West Africa.[1] A great deal of attention was paid to the various reformist groups, but much time also was spent considering ways in which to improve work among the African conscripts in the several colonial armies. Fenner Brockway, who met Padmore at a later date and was much impressed with him, describes this aspect of revolutionary work as 'encouraging the growth of the demand for political independence and stimulating among the native conscripts the idea that when a suitable opportunity came they should fight for their own national freedom'.[2] Padmore's stubborn persistence in this view angered many of his associates over the years.

The RILU, influenced by this conference, passed a "Special Resolution on Work among Negroes in the US and the Colonies" at its Fifth Congress, in March 1931. In the previous January, its new arm, the International Trade Union Committee of Negro Workers (ITUC-NW), began to issue the monthly *Negro Worker* (the first two issues of which were called the *International Negro Workers' Review*). It was printed at 8 Rothesoodstrasse in Hamburg, a decayed waterfront district destroyed during the Second World War. The house, according to persons who knew it, had been converted into a seamen's club, both to conceal the press and to facilitate contact with black sailors, who were targets and principal distributors of the periodical. After the dissolution of the German Communist Party (KPD), the house was taken over by a missionary society, which was fitting since copies of the *Negro*

Worker had been bound into religious tracts in order to pass police scrutiny.

Hamburg was a stronghold of the KPD, the residence of its president, Ernst Thaelmann, and a world port. There, in working-class Altona, the KPD's defence chief, Ernst Vollweber, led his men to battle with the Nazis. With luck, copies were carried aboard ships in bulk by the politically sympathetic dockers, but more often it was a matter of an individual sailor buying a copy and smuggling it into his locker. As with most clandestine publications, the editors relied upon multiple readership. A. A. Zusmanovitch, today a lecturer at Russia's Africa Institute, was at that time 'on mission' in Hamburg and has described some parts of the operation to Rolf Italiaander, recorded in *Schwarze Haut im Roten Griff*. He pointed out to the German writer that 'it was the very first international journal for the Negro in all continents, which was concerned with his troubles, needs and pains. What he had been dreaming of, an international platform for discussion, we Communists established for him.' J. W. Ford, the first editor, lasted only until the summer and then was replaced by Padmore. This may have been a simple matter of sending a professional to do the job, or there may be some substance to the tale that Ford was compromised by the police and had to be removed.[3] One of Padmore's last acts in Russia was to denounce American racism at a Leningrad Fourth of July rally in defence of the Scottsboro boys. He spoke as a representative of the United States Communist Party.[4]

In the early months of 1930, Padmore was moved to Vienna. Although it had been decided that the German port of Hamburg was his most logical base for work among seamen, there arose the problem of giving an officially acceptable reason for his being in the Weimar Republic. Austria, at that time, contained many political emigrants, especially from Eastern Europe.

The Communist Party of Austria was very small (and without political influence), but it had good connections among the intellectuals, and persons entirely devoted to the cause of communism placed themselves at the disposal of the communist 'apparatus'. . . . Communist activities were viewed with tolerance by the Austrian police (which was in the hands of the Social Democrats or such Christian Socialists who were imbued with liberal traditions). There was much more freedom of action for communists in Vienna than, for example, in Berlin and therefore different branches of the CI, the RILU, the IRA [International Red Aid—the organisation for assistance of revolutionaries], etc., used Austria as bases for their activities (to say nothing of different intelligence services which operated there). The idea of placing Padmore there originated in the difficulties he had to get legally into Germany.[5]

One of the Comintern men Padmore had met during his first Moscow visit was Y. Berger, who specialised in Near Eastern work. In May 1930, Berger was on his way back to Moscow from Syria by way of Vienna, where he was to receive instructions and documents. While in the Austrian capital, he was told of a young Negro he might wish to meet. To his surprise, it was Padmore who greeted him in a small flat in the Second District. He was living with an Austrian comrade and her two children, seemed much thinner, was shabbily dressed and obviously not happy in his circumstances.

Padmore's main complaint was that he felt isolated in Vienna. His language was English and his German was extremely inadequate at that time. He received newspapers which were dated on arrival . . . but had no contact whatsoever with things around him. He was given orders, by the organisation under whose auspices he was working in Vienna, not to meet with other comrades too frequently and not to make casual acquaintances in the boulevards or in cafés. As to this, incidentally, I heard from members of the team that Padmore's behaviour was exemplary . . . his behaviour was very modest compared to many other 'transit men' from the Balkans and the Near East, [some of whom] drank, squandered money, and caused all kinds of mishaps.[6]

Padmore impressed Berger as one of the most responsible colonials he had met. Padmore believed in 'independence now'; he could of course use 'the current ideological coinage but he was not content to do this [and was] searching for new, independent and even original paths'. Berger soon learned that for Padmore imperialism meant British imperialism. He was uninterested in American problems; indeed, he differentiated himself from some of the black American comrades who were obsessed with American questions. He always meant British colonies when Africa was being discussed. 'I do not remember his ever mentioning the French or Portuguese colonies.' At that time, Padmore insisted that the working classes everywhere were natural allies in the anti-colonial struggle, but he also told Berger that there were young African intellectuals at British universities who yearned for advice and aid.

A few days later Berger was ordered home.

Padmore remained in Vienna—we did not arrange to meet again or to correspond. At our last meeting, Padmore spoke of his doubts about his stay in Vienna. He maintained that from the point of view of his own personal security his stay in Vienna was desirable since it enabled him to work in peace. But is this activity worthwhile? George asked me that if I met the people directing the activities of the colonial peoples, and if I was asked what I thought of the continuation of the operation, to make clear to them 'that Vienna was too remote from revolutionary centres'.[7]

They did not meet again until 1958, and though Berger's career in the interval was equally astounding (he survived over twenty years of labour camps), it can form no part of this book. Whatever Berger may have passed along to the Comintern directors, nothing was done about Padmore's position until the next year, when the *Negro Worker* appeared in Hamburg at the ITUC-NW offices.

1931 was the year of Liberian–American and Liberian–League of Nations conflict. The new editor and secretary of ITUC-NW denounced American imperialism, saw the Firestone concession as a new phase of imperial rivalry, and rejected the Christy–Johnson–Barclay Commission's exculpation of the rubber company's labour policies. He added Dr Charles S. Johnson and the journalist George Schuyler to his list of 'good Negroes', the one for joining a whitewash commission, the other for condemning Liberia in the Negro press. Negro workers were warned against a perfect catalogue, a *Who's Who* of the Negro world: Garvey, Blaise Diagne, DuBois, Pickens, Walter White, A. Philip Randolph, Schuyler, Kelly

Miller, Robert Moton and Oscar de Priest.[8] Padmore was con
vinced that the actions of the Americo-Liberians proved the weak-
ness of Garvey's thesis that a black bourgeoisie should be trained.[9]
He later wrote: 'I have always considered it my special duty to
expose and denounce the misrule of the black governing classes in
Haiti, Liberia and Abyssinia, while at the same time defending
these semi-colonial countries against imperialist aggression.'[10]

Padmore skirted very close to the race conflict line in these
months. It was difficult to avoid racial references, of course, when-
ever labour and capital in a tropical setting were discussed, but
Padmore on occasion appeared to be stressing the whiteness of
capitalists. In a pamphlet entitled "What Is the International
Trade Union Committee of Negro Workers?", published in
Hamburg late in 1931, he talked principally of white robbers and
their black puppets, while at the same time maintaining that the
purpose of his committee was to build up Negro unions along
class rather than race lines.

During his first year with the committee, Padmore wrote six of
the organisation's twenty-five pamphlets* and many of his essays
were reprinted in the journals of various overseas parties. Padmore's
strength was his indefatigable nature, remarkable memory and
sense of organisation. He was able to state his aims concisely, he
collected statistics avidly, read the capitalist press in detail and
quoted from the generally accepted academic sources when he
touched upon sensitive issues. The best known of these works was
his famous *Life and Struggles of Negro Toilers*, the back cover of
which showed a gigantic Negro hovering over the United States,
the West Indies and Africa, snapping the links in the slave chain
which connected these distant places. (A modification of this figure
can be seen in the recently suppressed Ghanaian journal *Voice of
Africa*.) His 126-page book contained an amazing amount of
information on the condition of black men in three continents,
described their various organisations, showed statistical tables of
the black man's role in the various militaries of the great powers
(including the United States), and explained the role of the new

* *What Is the International Trade Union Committee of Negro Workers?*;
Life and Struggles of Negro Toilers; *Negro Workers and the Imperialist
War*; *Forced Labour in Africa*; *American Imperialism Enslaves Liberia*;
and *Labour Imperialism and East Africa*.

section of the RILU. The book, though on occasion lapsing into jargon, is in the main straightforward journalism which conveys a feeling that the black men of the world are at last awake, with the appropriate weapon of their deliverance at hand. Of his ten books or extended pamphlets, this and his last, *Pan-Africanism or Communism?*, published in 1956, are probably the best known. Though other functionaries of great repute such as Ralph Palme-Dutt, Harry Gannes and Alexander Losovsky also published for the committee that year, none produced anything more valuable than *Life and Struggles* . . . , which colonial governments banned immediately.[11]

One amusing anecdote about the later fortunes of this book perhaps should be preserved. When Padmore was expelled from the Comintern, *Life and Struggles* . . . naturally became an unbook and was withdrawn from circulation wherever possible. Considerable stocks remained in the basement of the Communist Party bookshop in London. For a time in the late 1930s the success of the Left Book Club was such that Victor Gollancz had no space in which to store his monthly offerings. Finally, he began to use the warehousing facilities of the party, at which point the party decided to move to expanded premises. During the move, a great many volunteers helped. One day, Padmore was told by his friend Gerald Kingscott, a railway dining-car attendant, that a young fellow-traveller down from Oxford was looking after the shop during lunch hours. Padmore and Kingscott got together what money they could, commissioned a taxi to wait around the corner till summoned and, with some trepidation, entered the store. After a suitable pause they asked after that marvellous book, so popular among coloured workers, *Life and Struggles* . . . . It was unknown to the eager student, nor was it on his shelf list. When they suggested that perhaps a copy might be in the basement, the young man professed ignorance of the lay-out and invited them to search, which they did, quickly discovering a large stock. The student, pleased to make so large a sale at ninepence a time, saw them whistle up their cab, bundle the books inside and depart. Precisely what the store managers thought when they learned of this transaction may be surmised. In subsequent years Padmore was able from time to time to sell copies at advanced prices. Today, a copy sells for five pounds.

If Liberia was important to him, so was South Africa. Whether he went there in disguise, as Russell Warren Howe has reported,[12] is difficult to say; but certainly he was familiar with the literature on that unhappy country and generally had an article about it in each issue of the *Negro Worker*. One of his 'specialist' contributors on South African affairs was Professor Ivan Potekhin, then a student of Padmore's age at Kutvu (1930–32), who, in the period 1932–35, wrote for the *Negro Worker*, using both his own name and occasionally the pen-name John Izotla. One presumes that he met Padmore at the university, though he did not say so in his interview with Italiaander.[13]

Padmore's peculiar effectiveness as a pamphleteer comes across very nicely in *Negro Workers and the Imperialist War—Intervention in the Soviet Union*. Here he ridiculed Garvey, the decayed bombast who had captured a seat on the Kingston (Jamaica) Municipal Council, reproved that 'petty bourgeois Negro intellectual' Dr DuBois for his reflexive anti-communism, and attacked Blaise Diagne as a black supporter of French imperialism. Garvey's entire movement by this time had collapsed: he had appealed to the League of Nations for Negro control of one of the former German territories, and his 'radical petty bourgeois national movement' was thoroughly penetrated by rogues, police agents and communists. In America, for example, his African Blood Brotherhood had a communist faction composed of the redoubtable Richard B. Moore, Otto Huiswood and Cyril Briggs.[14]

That the activities of the ITUC-NW were not clearly apprehended by the colonial authorities is suggested by an intelligence report which London sent to the Nyasaland government in June 1931, reporting on a meeting supposedly held in Berlin on May 14, where communists concerned with Africa had decided to entrust great responsibility to the 'Kibanist' organisation, whose representative was one Koniat. The Colonial Office was puzzled at this information. They thought, rightly, that Koniat might be Garan Kouyaté, but were baffled by his organisation, correctly deciding that the word was not a mis-spelled version of Kikuyu. One gathers that Simon Kimbangu and events in Lower Congo were unknown to them.[15] Those familiar with the lack of co-operation among the colonial powers will not be surprised. In fact, in May, the executive committee of the LAI did meet in Berlin. Forty-six attended, including '15 from colonial countries' and '15 from the oppressed nations and national minorities'. Padmore was elected to the General Council as a West Indian delegate: he never served as a brevet American again.[16] At the conclusion of the conference on June 2, delegates affirmed their belief that blacks throughout the world were attaining class consciousness, but especially so in the United States and South Africa.[17] From September, the LAI began issuing the bi-monthly *Anti-Imperialist Review* in German and English.

This was an intensive summer for the Comintern colonial specialists. In late June the International Labour Office (ILO) held a conference at Geneva to discuss colonial child welfare, billed as the "Save the Children" conference in left circles. Seven black persons attended unofficially, including J. W. Ford for the LAI and the ITUC-NW. Ford found the other blacks insipid: two were teachers, one a Gold Coast lawyer, another a law student in London, yet another from a Negro American fraternal order, while the last represented an East African organisation but lived in London (Jomo Kenyatta, one presumes). Ford denounced the assembly in a 'maximum demands' speech on the second day, charging that the evils the conferees talked of were the inevitable product of the colonialism their own governments promoted. The population of Africa was being destroyed through the neglect of health services and the atrocities committed upon forced labourers by capitalists and their Colonial Office supporters. So far as the Negroes of this earth are concerned, said Ford, all evils may be attributed to imperialist exploitation. The speech, which was given great publicity in communist circles,[18] further enhanced Ford's reputation as a Negro militant. It was reproduced as a penny pamphlet in the United States Communist Party's *Negro Problem* series, with the title "Imperialism Destroys the People of Africa".*

In his pamphlet explaining what the ITUC-NW was, Padmore had remarked that the communists and revolutionary seamen and dockers of Hamburg protected the committee. The defences were imperfect, for the December issue of the *Negro Worker* reported that the police had raided the offices of both the ITUC-NW in

---

* In such sensational circumstances, the lecture on African history which Professor Emil Torday, the noted Africanist, delivered to the delegates must have seemed somewhat lacklustre, despite the novelty of the subject.

Hamburg and the LAI in Berlin, in the process confiscating 10,000 copies of pamphlets at 8 Rothesoodstrasse. The Comintern was persuaded, perhaps rightly, that the Weimar government was seeking to curry favour with the British and French by agreeing to harry anti-colonial organisations.

Of the early months of 1932, little, apart from his editorship of the journal, is known about Padmore. His net expanded until it held about 4,000 people throughout the colonial world. He helped organise and attended the first dockers' and seamen's conference in Hamburg that May, where an International of Seamen and Harbour Workers (ISH) was formed; and he called for more efforts to acquaint colonial peoples with their lot and with the aims of the ITUC-NW. Valtin, on page 280 of *Out of the Night*, makes one tantalising reference to a Trinidad Negro, long resident in London, who attended this conference as the representative of the Mississippi river workers. Anyone familiar with this period and this sort of conference will agree that the tale is conceivable. The leader of the French Seamen's Federation at this Altona conference was Garan Kouyaté, who has been mentioned before and will be referred to again. This handsome young man reported on colonial conditions, but he was given little time and, by general agreement, his was the poorest section of the conference.[19] Padmore and he became close friends. He led a delegation to the American Embassy in Paris that November while the United States Supreme Court considered the Scottsboro appeal. Nancy Cunard records that he recalled the chargé d'affaires 'showed the utmost surprise at Negroes talking correct French'.[20]

That year in London Padmore also met C. A. Smith, later at various times chairman of the Independent Labour Party and the Common Wealth Party and editor of *Controversy*. Smith, according to his recollection, attended a socialist gathering and noticed two Negroes laughing uproariously. They turned out to be Padmore and James,* trading stories illustrative of the Comintern

* James, according to the version offered by Ivar Oxaal in *Index*, No. 2, University of Hull, Autumn 1965, had been invited to hear a speech 'a great Negro Communist' was giving. To his surprise this turned out to be his boyhood friend. Another source has it that only James's well-developed Trotskyism saved him from recruitment to Moscow. Padmore was in the British capital in September. See Samuel Rohdie, "The Gold Coast Aborigines Abroad", Vol. VI, No. 3, *Journal of African History*, 1965, p. 396.

zigzags. Padmore introduced himself as being in charge of all the world's Negroes, which Smith thought quite a parish. A diocese, rather, Padmore replied. Later, in a more serious vein, Padmore explained the double revolution: the first revolution was a racial one aimed at white imperialists, during which the Communist Party would collaborate with the local national bourgeoisie; the second was a class-based one to be organised by the party shortly after the first revolution had put local rulers in power.[21]

That autumn, in Paris, Padmore first met a remarkable woman with whom he had corresponded voluminously about Negro matters: Miss Nancy Cunard. She had recently returned from her celebrated trip to Harlem in pursuit of material for her huge book on Negro life. Padmore was only one of a large number of persons she had contacted in this connection, but, according to her, he became one of the two most important collaborators in the enterprise.[22] In the event, Padmore contributed four articles (reprints, mostly from *Life and Struggles* . . .) to her *Negro Anthology*, which was published in London in 1934.

Miss Cunard, the daughter of Sir Bache and Lady (Maude) Cunard of the shipping family, was a highly original character. She probably was fairly portrayed in Aldous Huxley's *Point Counter Point,* in which she appears as Lucy Tantamount. A rebellious young woman in conflict with her American mother (a Californian with views on race relations), she went to Paris permanently after her marriage ended in divorce. There she was intimate with members of the surrealist group, especially with Louis Aragon. She established the Hours Press, and was the first publisher of Samuel Beckett. Then, in 1928, in Venice she met and fell in love with the Negro American composer and pianist Henry Crowder, and it was he who introduced her to the world of Negroes. She soon became proficient in their slang, their dances, their quarrels and intrigues, and a passionate supporter of 'race' causes, in the process finally breaking with her mother. Through Padmore, she became the British organiser of funds for the Scottsboro boys in 1931 and 1932, which brought her into touch with International Labor Defense and the Negro American Communist Party attorney, William Patterson. She conceived the idea of publishing a book which would illustrate the condition of Negroes throughout the world. In this enterprise, Padmore was her principal contact. 'It was

Padmore who, even before we met, put me in touch with many coloured writers and personalities.'[23] To gather material, she came to New York with Crowder in the spring of 1932, where she scandalised the white (especially the Hearst) press by staying up in Harlem and consorting almost solely with Negroes and friends of Negroes. The recipient of remarkable abuse wherever she went,* she nevertheless collected a great many items and was promised contributions by all sorts of artists. 'Returning to London the next year', her obituary in the London *Daily Telegraph* says, 'Miss Cunard organized a mixed dance of Whites and Negroes. It electrified conventional society at the time.'[24] She also brought suit for libel against the British press, which had followed her affairs in both Americas with considerable interest, for, though she had broken with her family and was not an heiress, she was a Cunard. Her little privately printed pamphlet against her mother, "Black Man and White Ladyship", was circulated at the time and caused considerable titillation. (A copy is in the New York Public Library; others are available at high prices.)

Her book, offered at 42/-, appeared in February 1934. Wishart published it at her expense, the cost running to £1500, most of which came from the damages awarded her in various suits against newspapers. It was an outsize folio of sorts, with over eight hundred pages containing contributions from 150 persons, replete with drawings and photographs. The general tone, if it could be said to have a political as opposed to a moralist message, was communist. That is, the editor supplied a communist vocabulary to connect the many articles which themselves had no such orientation. The pieces which she herself contributed were interesting in the extent to which they reflected the views of the *Negro Worker* (which is excerpted heavily throughout). So, with respect to the NAACP, she could write that DuBois and his associates

---

* Some of the more virulent specimens she published in her book as "The American Moron and the American of Sense—Letters on the Negro". 'I should like to print all the raving, illiterate, anonymous letters', she explained. 'Some are very funny indeed, mainly from sex maniacs one might say—but what is to be done? They are obscene, so this portion of American culture cannot be made public.' They were very odd: threats from "x22" and the "Caucasians of America", and a mad letter from "Southern Woman" who insisted that Negroes controlled the United States.

failed or refused to recognise that the Negro question was an economic one and, as International Labor Defense charged, played down the actual number of lynchings each year by counting only those investigated, which were the acts of mobs. 'It is, however, the International Labor Defense, a non-partisan organisation fighting for the rights of white and black workers alike, and undertaking the defense of such monstrous cases of race hate and class struggle as the Scottsboro case . . . that has taken the very steps (which were proposed for the NAACP in 1912) announced by DuBois in his Atlanta speech.'[25] She was especially indignant that the NAACP had split with the ILD. 'Between Communists and Negroes the race barriers are down forever; at last, long last, white and black stand united. To recognise this fact it is not necessary to be a Communist, but to realise and not admit it is perforce to be a liar.'[26] In short, DuBois represented a small class of Negroes who themselves were well off, but they preserved this precarious dignity by being white men's niggers, by deluding the black masses into believing that they were free under existing circumstances. 'We call this spirit treachery.'[27]

The 'entrenched Negro leadership', as the communists usually referred to those whom the whites called principal Negroes, was on the defensive, according to this analysis. Such views as that expressed by the editor of the Atlanta *World*: 'This race is slow to change. It would prefer keeping its present status, no matter how low, than fly to a system, no matter what its worth, that is constantly lambasted by press and radio', were ridiculed by the communists, who saw the 'misleaders' as 'naturally terrified'. 'The politicians, utilizing Oscar De Priest [Negro Congressman from Chicago's South Side] as their spokesman, warn Congress that *they* will not be responsible if, through Congressional indifference and neglect, black voters turn Red. The preachers shout to the masses that Communism is an illegitimate child of Satan. The professional class begs the workers to realize that only through creating a strong middle class can the race "find" itself', wrote Eugene Gordon. But it was all too late. Only one course remained for them. 'Having vainly entreated Yahveh to reveal the secret of changing Red blacks into the ordinary, simple-minded blacks they originally were, entrenched Negro leadership gloomily bows its head, mournfully rolls its eyes, and mutters resignedly:

"Brethren, only one course is open to us, and that is the course this leadership has pursued since emancipation. We must continue to pursue it to the bitter end. Brethren, while there remains an opportunity for us to do so, let us prey." '[28] There is much more good stuff in this marvellous volume, but little so amusing, the communists not generally going in for humour.

The list of her contributors impresses: Langston Hughes, William Pickens, Zora Neale Hurston, William Carlos Williams, Arthur Schomburg, Alain Locke, Franklin Frazier, Rayford Logan, James Ivy, W. E. B. DuBois, Walter White, Theodore Dreiser, Arna Bontemps, Countee Cullen, William Plomer, J. J. Rabearivalo, Georges Sadoul, M. Herskovits, Norman Douglas, Nnamdi Azikiwe, George Schuyler, Raymond Michelet and George Padmore. It was a remarkable production, the result of two years' labour, a monument to an extraordinary woman.[29]

1933 was Hitler's year, and the German Communist Party soon felt it. By June, the *Negro Worker* was operating out of a post office box in Copenhagen, its files destroyed, its offices confiscated and many of its people in jail, among them Padmore.* Accounts of his imprisonment vary greatly. He was held from three to six months by the city police, who took some time to be thoroughly nazified, a factor of great importance to Padmore, who even so seems to have had a bad time of it. Finally, he was deported on his British passport and arrived on the east coast of England, where he was met by Special Branch officers. The authorities were troubled by his presence, but had no legal grounds on which to proceed against him. Though the *Negro Worker* was banned in the colonies, it could not be held up at home. There was a legal Communist Party in Britain, and so Padmore moved about the capital city of the principal enemy, mostly in the company of blacks, here making contact with Miss Cunard's friend, Chris Jones, Barbadian president of the Colonial Seamen's Association, there making arrangements for the *Negro Worker* to continue its precarious existence. It was a lean year and not much of Padmore appears on the record.

* Another was Padmore's close friend Edgar André, 'my teacher who fell in the struggle', to whose memory he dedicated his third book *Africa and World Peace*. André was beheaded in Hamburg on November 5, 1936. See *New Leader*, November 13, 1936.

It was a terminal year, though. His expulsion notice was not
served by the Comintern Control Commission until June 1934,
but this was the final statement of a fact accomplished much
earlier. Though in Miss Cunard's book, which appeared in
February of that year, Padmore was described as the secretary of
the ITUC-NW, by that time the office itself was moribund. The
internal history of the Comintern remains unclear, but, in the mid-
1930s, anti-colonial activity was reduced in favour of certain moves
calculated to gain Russia a greater degree of acceptance in the
West. The advent of Hitler speeded this development. In August
1933, the Comintern decided to disband the ITUC-NW, an organisation particularly odious to the western powers. Padmore, when
he learned of the decision on August 13, immediately resigned his
offices. There was no public reaction until the following April,
when the first reports of his anti-party activity appeared in print.
It is possible that the Comintern tried to regain his allegiance: he
was invited, according to his friends, to come to Moscow to justify
his conduct, but declined unless suitable safeguards and publicity
were guaranteed.

Many versions of his defection have appeared, but I think the
most likely one is his own, which he later printed twice. He had
been holding:

a responsible position in the higher councils of the Communist
International, which was called upon not only to endorse the
new diplomatic policy of the Soviet Government, but to put a
brake upon the anti-imperialist work of its affiliate sections and
thereby sacrifice the young national liberation movements in
Asia and Africa. This I considered to be a betrayal of the fundamental interests of my people, with which I could not identify
myself. I therefore had no choice but to sever my connection
with the Communist International. I formulated my position
quite clearly in a political statement which I submitted to the
Comintern Executive, and which was subsequently published
by the Negro Press, so that my case would be put before my own
people. With that the matter was closed as far as I was concerned, and I have never permitted my political objectivity in
regard to the Soviet Union to be influenced by my experiences
with the Comintern. These are the circumstances in which I

resigned from the Communist International, and it is only necessary to add that, in keeping with communist practice, a formal statement of my expulsion followed. But this did not disturb me in the least, for no one whose disassociation from the communist ranks might give rise to any political embarrassment is allowed to make his exit without vilification. Sometimes you are a 'Trotskyist', other times a 'left-wing deviationist', or a 'right-wing deviationist', depending upon the particular period; but I got away with it lightly, as my sin was merely 'petty bourgeois nationalist deviation'.[30]

It is a pity that Padmore's detachment was not exercised more often, for he could be amusing on this score. His nephew, Malcolm Luke, a London physician, who died recently while still a young man, once told me how Padmore used to recount receiving directives to cease attacking French, then British, then American imperialism, till he was left finally with the Japanese alone. These Asians, he snapped in disgust, are not the imperialists who have their boots across the black man's neck.[31] Years later, during the breathless period following Khrushchev's revelations to the cpsu's Twentieth Congress, Padmore wrote that the British Communist Party 'is fast becoming truly English in language. It has dropped the old Muscovite jargon in the *Daily Worker* and can even quote the Bible against its opponents . . . soon Trotsky will be back in the history books.'[32]

Charles Woodson took over the secretaryship of the ITUC-NW. The *Negro Worker* resumed publication in May 1934, still in Copenhagen, with an editorial apology for the disruption because of 'serious technical difficulties, editorial shortcomings [a reference to Padmore] and the necessity to change our location . . .'. Woodson was an undistinguished man, the author of a fanciful effusion *How to Organize and Lead the Struggles of the Negro Toilers* (published in Copenhagen in June 1935) which reads like diluted Padmore. He in turn soon gave way to the British Guianan, Otto Huiswood. If Padmore had fallen from on high, the *Negro Worker* itself was in a perilous state as well. In August 1934, the ITUC-NW was forced to leave Denmark and relocate in Brussels. But the Belgians too ejected them, and the October–November issue emanated from the offices of the Harlem *Liberator*. In 1935, they again managed to return to Copenhagen; then, in March 1936, a year before the magazine's demise, they moved to a final home in Paris.

Three consecutive issues of 1934 carried the anticipated attacks upon Padmore. His formal expulsion by the International Control Commission, dated February 23, 1934, complained that Padmore had refused to give up his friendship with Kouyaté, 'the expelled provocateur', lived in the apartment of one Jacques, also a provocateur, while repeatedly denying the same, worked openly for national bourgeois organisations on behalf of Liberia, argued for Negro unity on race rather than class lines, and in general displayed an incorrect attitude towards the nationalities question.[33] The new editor was incensed that Padmore, who formerly denounced the Americo-Liberians, had turned into 'one of the most zealous organizers of the Roosevelt–[W.M.] Jones "Committee of Aid" '.

In July, the editorial entitled "A Betrayer of the Negro Liberation Struggle" pointed out that everywhere the capitalists use the same devices to penetrate black liberation movements. Padmore now was unmasked as an agent, a petty bourgeois nationalist capable of ignoring the imperialist role of the United States in Liberia, the expounder of the absurd view that white men cannot understand Negro psychology: in short, a racist. He was attempting, in association with such persons as Professor DuBois, whom he formerly castigated for obsessive anti-communism, to raise $5 million to bail out the Liberian rulers, on the mistaken premise that reform could come from within a corrupt capitalist class. The same fraudulence attended the efforts of Gandhi and Garvey. But this was not all. Padmore also had given the German police the names of seamen who had co-operated with the ITUC-NW. 'He is branded as a filthy scoundrel, as a betrayer of the struggles of the Negro masses. But for serving his white masters so faithfully he must pay. The working class will not forget who are their friends and who are their enemies.' The charge that Padmore supported Liberia had a certain merit; in 1934, he wrote to DuBois: 'Liberia has her faults, but since white politicians are no better than black ones, it is our duty to save the "black baby from the white wolves".'[34]

In August, Helen Davis said the final words before Padmore

became an unperson to the *Negro Worker*. Her essay, "The Rise and Fall of George Padmore as a Revolutionary Fighter", declared that the proletariat seeks allies everywhere. Some of these allies fall through impatience, others are betrayed by their own social background. Padmore was a case in point, as some of his recent utterances proved. He had equated imperialism with the white race and seemed to be willing to press for the freedom of colonies instead of the freedom of colonial workers. His present tendencies were foreshadowed in the August 1933 issue of the *Negro Worker*, where he said that the future of Africa was a future for black men, while that of Europe was one for white men. Now he had begun to charge that communists had used the Negro masses. 'But the great masses of toilers are already set in motion, Padmore—you are but a little ant caught between two great forces.' Not all of this acrimonious writing reflected personal attitudes, of course. Zusmanovitch, according to Italiaander, said that the Profintern 'often received complaints from Hamburg concerning Padmore's obstinacy. I am sure he wanted to be a good communist, but he never knew much about teamwork between himself and members of the lower working class. . . . Yes, and then about his political attitude! In June 1934 he was expelled from the Communist Party and removed from his duties. I myself regretted this because I liked him.'*

An amusing confusion between Padmore and a young Liberian of the same name (today a senior member of his country's diplomatic service) was perpetuated by both Russia and the colonial powers. The Liberian was refused entry to the Gold Coast at this time, and, according to Legum, was traduced for over twenty years by the communists.[35]

Padmore, who had moved to Paris with Kouyaté, spent these months at work on a book which ultimately became *How Britain Rules Africa*. In June 1934 he was with Nancy Cunard in her home near Vernon in the Eure (Normandy), where he 'spent all the day and half the night writing', Miss Cunard recalled, 'and most of the hours of the day I typed for him, from his rather difficult handwriting. . . . His capacity for sheer, lengthy hard work was very great, and his knowledge seemed to me immense.'[36]

* English translation from Italiaander's book, *Schwarze Haut im Roten Griff*.

This silence under attack marked Padmore as a different sort of ex-communist than many. Zusmanovitch told Italiaander that he was sorry about Padmore's expulsion, apart from personal considerations, because he knew that life would stop for him, that he never could retrieve on the outside the sort of corporate security and sense of worth that he had known within the movement. This may have been the case with some (cf. *The God that Failed*), but not with Padmore. He refused to defend himself, except on rare occasions, mainly because he did not wish to provide ammunition for professional anti-communists, and because he continued to believe that only the Russians under communism had succeeded in decolonising and in eliminating manifestations of racial prejudice. He often told the following story, quoted here from *Left*, September 1941:

In 1930, while serving as a deputy on the Moscow Soviet, Losovsky, then secretary of the Profintern, asked me to serve on a commission investigating the conduct of some American engineers working on the construction of an automobile factory in Stalingrad. It was alleged that they had beaten up a Negro engineer named Robinson (I think he was a native of Jamaica) because they objected to a coloured man eating in the same restaurant with them! The men admitted the assault and offered to apologise to the Negro, but the Russian workers were so indignant at white men treating a fellow-worker in that fashion simply because of his race, that they demanded their immediate expulsion from the Soviet Union. The Americans were packed back to the United States and a warning issued to others to behave themselves. Could such a thing happen in 'democratic' Britain? The English people certainly have a lot to learn from the 'Godless' Russians.*

* This account varies somewhat from the contemporary newspaper versions. The attacked man was one Robert Robinson of New York City, a tool-maker, who, in the presence of other Americans, was beaten by two white southerners named Lewis and Brown who resented having a Negro receive equal, even preferential, treatment from the Russians. Their trial lasted six days; upon conviction they were sentenced to ten years' imprisonment. Both apologised, whereupon Lewis was deported and Brown, 'being deemed younger and less culpable, was pardoned by President Kalinin at the request of the Metal Workers' Union', and allowed

But, in October 1935, goaded by attacks in the Negro-American press and the *Daily Worker* (NY), Padmore did reply to his critics in the pages of *The Crisis*. There is some reason to accept the communist charge that his "Open Letter to Earl Browder" was composed earlier and held in abeyance. It is not necessary, though, to believe that its release was a crude attempt to slander the Soviet Union at a critical moment.[37] In any event, Padmore charged that the communists themselves had delayed their attack. After all, his last article on Liberia had been published in January 1932, so why had he not been criticised then? Indeed, why had they waited so many months after his resignation before beginning their slanderous campaign? In his only published utterance which sounds at all self-pitying, he said that he had given up his law career at the party's behest, had devoted eight honourable years to its affairs, built an organisation with thousands of members, only to have his integrity challenged by despicable people. J. W. Ford, for instance, had twisted an innocent article on Ethiopia, which he had contributed to Miss Cunard's *Negro Anthology*, into seeming like a sycophantic account of the emperor's greatness, all because Haile Selassie had been called 'a progressive monarch'.

Though Miss Cunard protested to the *Afro-American*, the damage was done.

A lesser man would likely have become a howling counter-revolutionary overnight. . . . As soon as my *Negro* came out in mid-February 1934 (and Ford, as contributor of an article, had automatically received his copy) there came to me an article, by him, purporting, you might think, to be some sort of review of the book. It was a diatribe only against Padmore in the *Afro-American*, entitled "Padmore Sups with Kings and Emperors". These 'kings and emperors' turned out to be Haile Selassie,

---

to remain in the Soviet Union (Bill Dunne in *New Masses*, September 1931; see also *Afro-American*, September 5, 1931). Robinson said that most American mechanics had left Russia, finding themselves unable to cope with such a different world. It was suggested at the trial that the morality of some Americans was deficient. Lewis and Brown remind one of the 'trial' the CPUSA held in the matter of Comrade Yokinen, a Finnish immigrant held liable for negrophobia. (See Howe, Irving, and Coser, Lewis, *The American Communist Party: A Critical History*, Beacon Press, New York 1962, pp. 209–10.)

because Padmore wrote a very good piece on Ethiopia for *Negro*, in which he called the Negus 'a progressive monarch'. I suppose that under orders (as yet unknown to Padmore) the word 'progressive' was enough.[38]

Ford also wrote for the CPUSA *Negro Problem* series "World Problems of Negro Peoples: A Refutation of George Padmore".

In July 1935, Miss Cunard was refused a visa to the Soviet Union, in her view because she had defended Padmore. Only the intervention of Louis Aragon and Homer Smith (though the latter does not remember) turned the trick. In Moscow, she met the CPUSA attorney, William Patterson, with whom she had worked on the Scottsboro case, 'and did not refrain from telling him full-square in what an appalling manner Padmore had been treated, denied the right to question accusation, to defend himself and to prove how untrue was the charge. Patterson just looked at me rather pitifully and said "Oh, Nancy...". Whereat we talked of other matters.' Only four years later Ford wrote that Haile Selassie's government 'while not yet democratic in the capitalist sense, was progressive in relation to the economic stage of the history of the country'.[39] But then times had changed.

Through all this Padmore remained silent about the charge concerning his association with the expelled Garan Kouyaté. In his most comprehensive account of this period, he mentioned the man only once: as a delegate to the 1927 Brussels conference who was shot by the Nazis when Paris was occupied in 1940.[40] This seems to be disingenuous. Kouyaté indeed was executed by the Germans, but at a later date in the occupation and, according to a tale which Miss Cunard attributed to Jules Monnerot (a Martiniquais close to the surrealists in the 1920s), for misappropriation of funds given him by the Germans for the production of propaganda. When one remembers that he had been expelled from the Communist Party, among other things, for embezzlement, the story makes sense, for the Germans tried hard to find Africans to attack French colonialism. Kouyaté, according to Miss Cunard, who met him about the same time she met Padmore, was a Bambara schoolmaster, an adept in written French, remarkable for his high-piled hairdo and tribal cicatrices. Padmore's attachment to the man remains unexplained, for Padmore was scrupulous about money matters and thoroughly law-abiding. His nephew recalled that the strongest epithet his uncle ever used was 'rascal', which he occasionally trotted out when black exploiters were being discussed. He was otherwise reluctant to publicise Negro shortcomings.

3

The Hard Years: Black Brothers in London

IN HER SAVAGE article, Helen Davis referred slightingly
to Padmore's attempts to start a journal and organise a conference.
She had in mind a projected Negro World Unity Congress, the
suggestion for which had come from a meeting of French Africans
in Paris early in 1934 under the leadership of Garan Kouyaté.
Padmore's comments are so interesting that they deserve quotation
at length from (perhaps) his earliest letter to Professor W. E. B.
DuBois:

> The French Negroes recently held a conference under the
> leadership of a young Sudanese [*sic*] whom you no doubt have
> heard about, Mr Garan Kouyaté, the editor of *La Race Nègre*.
> The Negro problem was discussed relative to the present econo-
> mic and social crisis the world over, and the fascist danger
> which threatens our racial extermination. It was the most
> serious political discussion which I have ever listened to among
> Negroes. The Conference decided to take the initiative to con-
> vene a Negro World Unity Congress, for the purpose of
> hammering out a common program of action around which
> world unity among the blacks can be achieved. The Negro students
> in Europe are demanding action. I also found this attitude very
> evident among the West African students when I was recently
> over in London.* I took the opportunity of informing the

* In London Padmore came to know members of the West African
Students' Union (WASU). To a degree uncommon for West Indians,

French Negroes about the work of the NACP [*sic*] and your work in connection with the Pan-African movement. They decided to invite your organization to participate in the Congress which has been fixed for the summer of 1935—providing the war-makers give us so much time. This is another question which is agitating the minds of French Negroes very much. For they have not forgotten how Diagne and other so-called leaders inveigled them into the last one, but this time they will have a wideawake youth to deal with. Will you help us in trying to create a basis for unity among Negroes of Africa, America, the West Indies, and other lands? We think it can be done, if men like you were to lend a hand. We read that Negro students in America are beginning to think of other things besides fraterni-ties, football and 'petting parties'. We welcome this. We would like to establish closer connections with these Negro student groups and organizations. Can you help us? Perhaps there are students in Atlanta University who will be interested in our efforts.[1]

This letter offers a variety of insights into Padmore's development. His essential pessimism about 'Negro' seriousness and sense of history frequently crops out in his private writings: according to his nephew, Padmore used to sigh about 'those Negroes' when vexed. His cynicism about the motives of middle-class Negro Americans was reinforced later in 1935 when a Dr Willis A. Huggins arrived from New York to raise funds for Ethiopia. He got in touch with WASU, which put him on to James's committee. The International African Friends of Ethiopia procured the neces-

---

Padmore could get along with these touchy students, who at the time were embroiled with the Colonial Office concerning a hostel which they wanted freed from official supervision. For a while they had used Aggrey House, 47 Doughty Street, which a West Indian physician, Dr Harold Moody, had placed at their disposal, until they learned that it was at least partially financed by the Colonial Office, and withdrew indignantly ("Truth About Aggrey House . . .", WASU pub., March 1934). Padmore's most important new West Indian contact in London was Dr Cedric Belfield Clarke, a physician, whose surgery at the Elephant and Castle became a gathering point for Negro and African activists. In later years, Clarke became Padmore's medical adviser and friend, attended him in his final illness and wrote a graceful obituary for *The Times*. (Interview, Clarke and author, September 1964.)

sary credentials from the Ethiopian Minister in London. And then Huggins disappeared.[2] On the other hand, his public utterances contain almost no human references—indeed, they are impersonal in a way which is quite striking. He was aware of this, and once remarked to his publisher and confidant, Dennis Dobson, that he put no Africans in his books, not because he was indifferent to them, but because he wanted nothing to get in the way of the main point—the indictment of colonialism on a sound academic basis. The letter also indicates how clear was Padmore's break with the Profintern by this date, and, by its lack of jargon and Aesopian language, suggests that he previously had written that way as a matter of convention rather than conviction.

At another point in this same letter, he wrote of *The Crisis*, to which he had sent an article: 'I used to receive your journal quite regularly when I was in Germany. But after my arrest and deportation by the fascists, I lost contact with it. I should be very glad to receive a copy of it for our political study circle of African emigrants here. Unfortunately, we cannot pay, for most of the fellows are unemployed.'

Padmore wrote this letter on the stationery of L'Union des Travailleurs Nègres, who proclaimed that 'L'Union Fait la Force', a wry message in 1934. It may have had some effect upon DuBois, however, for, in the same month, he sent out a letter of his own to dozens of Negro leaders, urging them to help organise a militant youth movement for the world liberation of coloured peoples. DuBois had outlined similar ideas at the conference held in Joel Spingarn's home in Amenia, New York, a year before, encountering resistance from some of the older NAACP leaders, a resistance which soon led DuBois to his first break with that body and into contact with the wider world of the new-style Pan-Africanists. By 1934, then, both DuBois and Padmore had arrived at a point where they could co-operate.[3]

Another conference to consider the Negro plight was called by the League of Coloured Peoples (LCP) at the Albert Hall in London on July 14 and 15, with the theme "The Negro in the World Today". About forty-three were present, without exception reformers who deplored conditions and called for a change of heart on the part of white men. They aroused only contempt in the world of militants. The LCP had been founded in 1931 by Dr Harold

Moody, a Jamaican with London medical qualifications, who ran his organisation from his home and surgery at 164 Queen's Road, SE15. Throughout his life, he tried to solve the race problem through the application of Christian principles, and continued to the end, despite growing evidence to the contrary, to hope the British public would come to love their black brothers. He occasionally co-operated with Padmore, as in 1938 when the Bledisloe Commission was examining the possibility of 'closer association' of the Rhodesias, but in general he preferred to associate with more respectable groups. Whereas, in the early war years, he argued that black men had a positive role in the British Empire, Padmore was convinced that, at least in Kenya, British settlers would prefer rule by Hitler to any form of African advancement.[4]

The main cause for Negro alarm was the worsening of Italo-Ethiopian relations. This was seen as yet another in the catalogue of aggressive acts perpetrated by whites upon their coloured brothers. It was neither Ethiopian nor communist policy, however, to identify the conflict as a racial one. Emperor Haile Selassie wanted money from Negro Americans, not volunteers—though, of course, bizarre individuals such as Hubert Fauntleroy Julian, the "Black Eagle" of aircraft barnstorming fame, did become a colonel in the imperial airforce.[5] The question, the emperor claimed, concerned the rights of small nations and the powers of the League of Nations. For the communists, J. W. Ford and the associate editor of the New York *Daily Worker*, Harry Gannes, argued nearly the same.[6]

Padmore moved to London permanently in 1935. There he contacted C. L. R. James, whom he had not seen since 1932. James was directing the ad hoc International African Friends of Ethiopia, a defence committee which tried to mobilise British opinion on behalf of that country. Together with a number of destitute West Indians, Padmore took rooms, first in the Vauxhall Bridge Road, then in Guilford Street near Russell Square. A British Guianan named Griffiths, better known by his adoptive Ethiopian style of T. Ras Makonnen, was the cook and business manager. A frequent caller and guest was a young student, Eric Williams, today Prime Minister of Trinidad and Tobago, who followed Padmore and James closely, but never joined their organisations, preferring instead to prepare for an Oxford First.

The present Ceylonese Ambassador in Russia, T. B. Subasinghe, who was close to Padmore for the decade ending in 1945, said that Padmore 'went through very difficult times in that period. He conducted political study classes for some colonial students, including myself. Those participating in the study classes made small contributions to pay him for his lectures. But these were very small sums of money.'[7] In a short time Padmore managed to meet most persons on the British non-Stalinist left: Fenner Brockway and F. A. Ridley of the ILP, Reginald Reynolds and his wife (the novelist Ethel Mannin), ex-Comintern workers such as Walter Goldwater (the American bookdealer and expert in Africana), and a host of others who had been with the LAI before it withered in the Popular Front period.[8]

With their usual blending of fact and innuendo, plus a little out of date biographical information, the Intelligence Services were on to him. In a secret circular sent out to the colonies, they advised that 'George Padmore, former secretary of the International Trade Union Committee of Negro Workers, has now formed, in conjunction with Tiemeko Garan Kouyaté, a prominent French Negro communist, his own organisation for revolutionary work in Africa, entitled the "Pan-African Brotherhood" ' and already had issued a manifesto on the Ethiopian crisis.[9] Unfortunately, there was no such body, Kouyaté no longer was a communist—important or otherwise—nor was Padmore in very close touch with him after leaving Paris for London. Still, things could be worse, as was evidenced by the receipt, by the editor of the *Nyasaland Times*, of a copy of the proceedings of the annual conference of the Negro Welfare Association. He passed it to the colonial government. Sir H. B. Kittermaster, the Governor, minuted: 'In British Honduras, I used continually to receive despatches from the CO [Colonial Office] dealing with this organisation. Have we none here?' There were none and neither the intelligence officer nor the superintendent of police 'had ever heard of it before'. The conference, which was held at Conway Hall on October 20, 1935, had noted with concern the spread of indirect rule in West Africa, especially in the Gold Coast, demanded freedom now, complained that unemployment among Negroes in Great Britain was nearly complete, protested that black students were unable to find accommodation and called for League of Nations sanctions against Italy and world solidarity in the Ethiopian cause. The Nyasaland government, now that it knew of the Association, placed its publications on the banned list.[10]

Padmore's concern over Ethiopia was evidenced in the first article which he did for *The Crisis*: in "Ethiopia and World Politics", published in the May 1935 issue, he called for all black men to aid the endangered empire. He was introduced to the readership as a free-lance writer living in Paris, which suggests that the new editor (P. Wilson) knew little of his author's movements since submitting the article.

After leaving the ITUC-NW, Padmore never again joined a non-Negro organisation, though he was closest to the Independent Labour Party. He refused to associate himself with the Ethiopian campaigns of other groups, such as the LAI and the Abyssinia League,[11] and, though very close to James, he did not become a Trotskyite or any other form of deviationist. However, his contempt for the British Communist Party was boundless. The police believed that 'his relations with the LAI and Reginald Bridgeman have for a long time been extremely acrimonious',[12] a relatively accurate depiction of the communist attitude, though insensitively ignorant of Padmore's inner condition.

A good illustration of this aloofness from white-controlled bodies with African interests is recorded in the pages of *East Africa and Rhodesia*, where the proceedings of a conference, called by the National Peace Council to discuss colonial questions, were reported.[13] The Council was concerned with the increasing probability that colonial issues might become sufficiently critical to lead to another war. Various speakers advocated that Britain place all its colonies, but especially the Crown colonies, under League of Nations mandate, not because this was in the best interests of Africans, but because it demonstrated British bona fides to other covetous nations and acted as a guarantee that Britain would not deprive these nations of African raw materials. As Sir Arthur Salter put it: 'In regard to raw materials there should be an international convention guaranteed by all Colonial Powers ensuring non-discrimination, the participation by consuming countries in the control of monopolies, and unrestricted supply in peace and war, except when the League imposed a blockade against an aggressor.' Leonard Barnes and Professor William

Macmillan spoke much more to the colonial peoples' brief, but even these men tended to talk of Africa as a European problem, as a piece of territory coveted by some white nations and controlled by others. The Reverend Leighton Richards went further: if they must talk about Africa for the Africans, then they might as well talk about returning the United States to the Indians and Australia to its aborigines. 'He drew attention to the successful administration of the International Settlement in Shanghai', which hardly commended itself to colonials.

The conference was finally rebuked by 'Mr John [*sic*] Padmore, an African representing the International African Friends of Ethiopia', who concluded the affair by reminding his auditors that 'you discuss the redivision of Africa to satisfy discontented nations like Germany and Italy, but the views and opinions of the Africans themselves are not solicited. It may have been nothing more than an oversight on your part, but it certainly does not establish much confidence among the people of Africa.' Padmore allowed that Africans wished to co-operate with their European friends, but this co-operation could not be that of horse and rider (an early use of a figure much employed by Lord Malvern of Rhodesia). And he was doubtful that handing colonies over to Geneva, so long as Geneva reflected only the views of the colonial regimes, would be very helpful to Africans.

There were, of course, a few British from the establishment who would have agreed with Padmore. He never met them. Major Arthur Victor Langton, a long-time member of the Royal African Society, urged that body to protest against Italian aggression, and was assured by the secretary, R. Nicholson, CMG, that members of the society's council were convinced that:

Such a course would be inadvisable as the Foreign Office would be pretty certain not to welcome it and the Society is moreover non-political. It is very true, as you remarked, that behind the political aspect of the matter there is the far larger issue of peace and freedom and native rights. I hope that the dispute may be settled without detriment to any of them, but I think that the Council of the Society would share the view that any action on our part at the present juncture might not be as helpful as it was designed to be.[14]

Black Revolutionary

At Arthur Ballard's Socialist Book Centre, Padmore first met F. A. Ridley, author of a pamphlet, "Mussolini over Africa", who provided entry into the leadership of the ILP. Though he never joined the ILP, Padmore wrote frequently for its journal, the *New Leader*,* edited by Fenner Brockway for many years, and became, in the estimation of Walter Padley, MP, during the later 1930s and the war years, one of the leading intellectuals in it. On several occasions, the ILP tried to get him to stand for election to parliament, without success.[15]

In 1937, Padmore spoke at the ILP Summer School for the first time, as he did henceforth most years until he left England for Ghana. A photo of him (see frontispiece), characteristically well-dressed, with a cigarette rather than the pipe which in later years customarily jutted from his mouth, survives the occasion of his debut as an ILP speaker. The party chairman, James Maxton, the fiercely independent Scottish member of parliament, took the photo, which looks as though some North London suburb was the venue. There is some mystery though, for it was posted to his boyhood friend Alex Symister from Oslo on October 20. This agrees with an account that Padmore travelled to Norway that year, in the process crossing Germany by rail. The reason for this visit is unknown.

In the following year Miss Cunard published *Authors Take Sides*, a collection of statements by 144 writers on the Spanish Civil War. Padmore, who saw her off to the war at the Gare d'Orsay in August 1936, contributed an article interesting for its consistency of view. 'The sympathy of all Africans and other colonial peoples naturally goes out to the toiling masses of Spain in their heroic struggle against Fascist barbarism, for they have not forgotten Abyssinia. And precisely because of this, it is so regrettable that democratic Spain, by failing to make an anti-imperialist gesture to the Moors, played into the hands of Franco. This should be a reminder to the European workers that: "No people who oppress another people can themselves be free".' He argued with extreme skill that when Europeans professed horror at General Franco's use of Moorish troops they were not only being inconsistent, since substantial numbers of blacks had been welcomed

* Ballard later wrote a "Round the Empire" column for this paper— see *New Leader*, February 10, 1939.

by the Allies during the World War, but also implicitly racist. Why should they be chilled at the thought of black troops? And did they not see that the black soldiers themselves were a function of imperialism, an aspect of exploited humanity?[16] (To his credit, George Orwell grasped this in his essay "Marrakesh", written in 1939.) In Reginald Bridgeman's opinion, Padmore did much to minimise the Moorish matter among British intellectuals on the left.[17]

In 1936, Padmore's second book, *How Britain Rules Africa*, appeared and received generally approving reviews.* The book was in the main a sober compendium, full of statistical tables and replete with descriptions. Padmore told plainly in manifold detail the way in which things actually were done in the British portions of the continent. He showed his mastery of government publications, as well as the polemical press, but erected no higher theory upon this base.

At an Indian Congress rally that year, Padmore met K. D. Kumria, the founder of Swaraj (Freedom) House in Percy Street. Through Kumria, he came into touch with many of the Indian Congress people in London. Padmore had been quite hostile to Congress during his Profintern days and retained a feeling that they were operating along the wrong lines—'He had a high regard for people like Jawaharlal Nehru and Subash Chandrabose. But as a Marxist at the time, he also pointed out the limitations of these leaders and of the Indian National movement which was under the dominant influence of the Indian bourgeoisie.'[18] He developed a warmth for individuals, especially Krishna Menon. Throughout his life Padmore displayed a talent for associating with people who detested each other, for Kumria and Menon were enemies, yet each knew and was fond of Padmore.[19] In succeeding years, especially after 1947, Swaraj House was used for the meetings of many African protest groups.

His third book, *Africa and World Peace* (with a foreword by Sir Stafford Cripps†), came out in 1937. It is rather a mélange of

---

* This was published in Switzerland as *Afrika unter dem Yoke des Imperialismus*; it is the only one of his works which appeared concurrently in translation.

† *International African Opinion*, September 1938, attacked Sir Stafford for his reactionary views on trusteeship. I do not know the explanation for Sir Stafford's approval of Padmore's text.

themes, with considerable reiteration throughout and certain inconsistencies. He suggested that Russia was, perhaps, indifferent to the Ethiopian position because the Italo-Ethiopian war was a racial one; yet, nevertheless, he called for colonial peoples to support the Soviet Union, which was 'motivated by a genuine desire for peace and not merely by political expediency'. The book called for an anti-fascist coalition and was an excellent exposition of the Hobsonian–Leninist view of Africa's significance to Europe. It was favourably reviewed on the left, though members of the ILP felt their role in the Spanish Civil War was not adequately discussed. As Reginald Reynolds pointed out, for several weeks in the summer of 1935, under Fenner Brockway, the ILP had called for worker sanctions against Italy, even if the party executive later changed the line to one of neutrality between two dictatorships. Weak as this was, no other group on the left had gone so far.[20]

Padmore maintained his Caribbean interests, producing in 1937, in association with a young student, Arthur Lewis, the pamphlet *The West Indies Today*.[21] There is, however, some doubt as to the extent of Padmore's contribution to this work. In 1965, Professor Lewis said: 'I do not think he had any hand in writing the pamphlet *The West Indies Today*. According to my recollection, I wrote it and he published it, through the organisation he was running at the time. It does not seem to be written in his style. However, this happened thirty years ago, so I cannot be fervently sure.'[22]

In 1937, Padmore met the woman who became known as his wife: Miss Dorothy Pizer, an Englishwoman who died in Accra in November 1964. This very bright North London girl had been too poor to accept a scholarship, so her formal education was limited, something she overcame through serious application to study. As she was a stenographer, it was natural that she should begin to offer to help an attractive man with similar political views and the glamour of worldly experience. This book was but the first of many typescripts and transcripts she produced in the next twenty-two years. From all accounts, their ménage had a constant stream of visitors, all of whom she coped with, cooked for and tolerated. If Peter Abrahams's fictionalised portrayal of Padmore (Lanwood in *A Wreath for Udomo*) is a cruel travesty, his version of Dorothy Pizer seems to square with others' observations. When the home they had established in St Bride's was bombed out in

1941, they moved to Cranleigh Street, NW1, where they lived until they moved finally to Ghana late in 1957. For most Africans, 22 Cranleigh House was the headquarters of anti-colonial agitation during the 1940s and 1950s.

In 1937, Padmore also established the International African Service Bureau (IASB) from the remnants of James's Ethiopian defence committee. The Bureau was a West Indian organisation and, apart from Padmore's own contacts with WASU and individual Africans such as Kenyatta, had little African support. Even Padmore's close friends were inclined to minimise the importance and potential of the IASB. Its motto was 'Educate, co-operate, emancipate. Neutral in nothing affecting the African people'; but some friendly observers thought these tasks too diffuse. 'The organization was formed in March 1937, and has possibilities for doing constructive work if it limits its field of endeavor, which at present seems too wide for effective work', as an American tourist wrote in the *Afro-American*.[23]

Their journal, *International African Opinion*,* began in July 1938 under James's editorship.† It was a well-produced threepenny magazine, nearly impossible to come by today. (Indeed, my examination has been limited to copies in the police files of various colonial archives.) The executive, of whose seven members only Kenyatta and I. T. A. Wallace-Johnson were African, saw the organisation as a ginger group which could stimulate the press to a greater awareness of colonial grievances. In this they were usually helped by Brockway, who from 1938 on placed a large number of IASB notices and Padmore essays in the *New Leader*, and C. A. Smith, who did the same in *Controversy*. The patrons of the Bureau were such well-known figures on the left as the Reverend Reginald Sorenson, D. N. Pritt, KC, Sylvia Pankhurst, Arthur Creech Jones and Victor Gollancz. After leaving 94 Gray's Inn Road the

---

* Two other ephemeral publications preceded *International African Opinion*. The first was *Africa and the World*, edited by Wallace-Johnson, who next, in association with Padmore, produced the *African Sentinel*. The police believed that the latter, begun October–November 1937, was produced with money supplied by Nancy Cunard. Shortly before her death, she vehemently denied (*a*) that she had had any, or (*b*) spent it for this purpose.

† James left for New York and a speaking engagement in October; he remained in the United States throughout the war.

Bureau used the offices of the ILP just before the war, and, in Padmore's person, became in effect the colonial section of that declining party.

Their stated aims may be summarised as agitational, educational and administrative. They demanded the abolition of onerous pass laws and taxes, insisted upon the right of Africans to organise pressure and interest groups, to receive equal pay for equal work, to publish, assemble and move about freely: in short, to possess 'democratic rights, civil liberties and self-determination'. Membership was open only to Africans and those of African descent, but associate membership could be obtained by others who sympathised with their aims and objects. 'One of the chief functions of the Bureau is to help enlighten public opinion particularly in Great Britain (and other democratic countries possessing colonies inhabited by Africans and people of African descent) as to the true conditions in the various colonies, protectorates and mandated territories in Africa and the West Indies.' They professed no desire to usurp or monopolise the field, but to 'co-ordinate and centralize the activities of the various organizations—be they political, Trade Union, Co-operative, Fraternal, Cultural, etc.— which at present exist in different parts of the black world, and in this way bring them into closer fraternal relations with one another, as well as sympathetic organizations in Great Britain and other countries, so as to arouse concerted action upon all questions affecting the common economic, political, social and educational well-being of the Africans and peoples of African descent.'[24]

Once again, the Intelligence people were only partly privy to colonial matters. A report, "Wallace-Johnson and the International African Service Bureau", insisted upon the Sierra Leonean's responsibility for creating the Bureau, a claim which those associated with the IASB never supported. It also referred to Padmore's 'Pan-African Brotherhood'.[25] Wallace-Johnson was much in the news at this time, which perhaps is why he was identified as being so very important in the Bureau. It is quite possible that his visit to Padmore in the late winter of 1937 triggered the decision to create the IASB, but Wallace-Johnson returned home in the next year—according to the police, over a money dispute within the Bureau's executive—and Padmore dominated it until its merger into the Pan-African Federation in 1944. Padmore's

Pan-African Brotherhood is unknown, but may be the unsuccessful little group which C. A. Smith thinks he recalls Padmore's having tried to start in Hampstead.[26]

Because at his accidental death, in the spring of 1965, he was a forgotten man, and whether or not he was as important as the police presumed, Isaac Theophilus Akkunna Wallace-Johnson does deserve some mention; with the exception of a brief notice in James Coleman's *Nigeria: Background to Nationalism*,[27] little scholarly attention has been paid to him recently. Born in Wilberforce, Sierra Leone, in 1895, he was a clerk in the Carrier Corps from 1916 to 1920, during which he saw a considerable part of Africa. Leaving the Corps, he went back to work for the Lever predecessor to the United Africa Company, and then entered government service. Blacklisted as a strike organiser, he went to sea for five years, during which he published the *Seafarer*, an occasional journal of labour news. In 1931, he founded the Nigerian Workers' Union, went to Moscow after attending the Negro Workers' Congress in Hamburg, and there studied at Kutvu, becoming a member of the ITUC-NW. He wrote for the *Negro Worker*—anonymously and as W. Daniels and Abdul Mohammed Afric.

In 1933, he went again to the Gold Coast where, within a month, he was arrested and deported for agitating about the Scottsboro case. From 1934 to 1936, Benjamin Nnamdi Azikiwe and he agitated effectively in the *African Morning Post*, both ultimately being arrested in June 1936 under revised press legislation for writing and uttering a seditious editorial: "Has the African a God?" Meanwhile, Wallace-Johnson had also organised the West African Youth League. He was convicted for sedition on October 18 and sentenced to a fine of £50 or three months in detention unless the fine were paid within fourteen days. In December, the West African Court of Appeal upheld the conviction, agreeing that under the new laws it was not necessary to incite to violence. Leave to appeal was granted in July 1938 and an appeal fund (with Lord Olivier as honorary treasurer) was organised. Upon Sir Stafford Cripps's application, Wallace-Johnson was allowed to appeal in *forma pauperis*. After an initial refusal, the Gold Coast government agreed to pay printing costs of £60. D. N. Pritt appeared for the appellant on the last two days of October 1939.[28] One of the sentences in the editorial which the Privy Council considered read in part: 'Send detectives to stay around the house of any African who is nationally conscious and who is agitating for national independence. . . .' The conviction was upheld, but the case was thought sufficiently important for some costs to be allowed the appellant from colonial funds.[29] Meanwhile, of course, Wallace-Johnson had been to England to organise his case, taken part in the foundation of the IASB, been re-arrested in Sierra Leone in 1937, and, at the outset of the war, been given one year's hard labour. On March 19, 1942, he was released into offshore island detention with his West Indian wife for the duration of the conflict. 'The Governor was satisfied that with a view to preventing his acting in a manner prejudicial to public safety it was necessary that he be detained', the order read. Pratt and Boyle, editors of Wallace-Johnson's paper, the *African Standard*, were arrested later for re-publishing an American criticism of the Privy Council ruling. Wallace-Johnson was released in late 1944 and immediately nominated to attend the forthcoming world trade union conference in London in February 1945. He also attended the foundation meeting of the World Federation of Trade Unions in Paris that September and was an effective colonial spokesman at both.[30]

Early in 1938, Padmore wrote the first of many articles for the ILP *New Leader*. In "Hands off the Colonies!" he said that war was inevitable in a capitalist, imperialist world. The Parliamentary Labour Party was a hopelessly reformist body; indeed, the only correct party (and only after the Ethiopian defeat) was the ILP.[31] In the estimation of his ILP colleague, the then organising secretary John McNair, Padmore 'was simply a genuine Socialist and therefore Libertarian and International. He was in complete opposition to all forms of totalitarianism, Nazi, Fascist and Stalinist. He also was naturally opposed to Imperialism but he considered it a lesser evil than totalitarianism. He said to me on several occasions, "Imperialism may be modified but Totalitarianism is the night to which there is no dawn." '[32] The real harm done by the present Communist Party line, Padmore wrote, was that it created a false dichotomy between so-called good and bad imperialisms.

On April 1, 1938, Padmore, Smith, McNair and Brockway spoke at an ILP course on "Imperialism and War"[33] in Essex Hall in

Essex Street. In the previous month Padmore had attacked the report of the commission appointed to enquire into the strikes and disorder in Trinidad during the previous summer. That a British trade unionist member of the commission, Sir Arthur Pugh, accepted the verdict which the colonial ruling class had settled against the Trinidad trade unionists 'only serves to make more difficult the task of colonial socialists in convincing coloured workers that they can expect help from official British Labour in their struggle for better economic and social conditions', he wrote disgustedly.[34]

That Empire Day (May 24) a large anti-colonial exhibition at Conway Hall was sponsored by the IASB and other like-minded organisations. J. F. Horrabin chaired and Padmore was one of four speakers. He talked of fascism in the West Indies and South Africa and called for British workers' aid. The *New Leader* already had run an Empire Special Edition[35] in which Padmore repeated his West Indian charge and Kenyatta discussed land in Kenya. (The famous photo of "Burning Spear" appeared, as it had on several other things in that year, including one of the IASB pamphlets written by Padmore.)

Later, in July, they decided to follow the Empire Exhibition in Glasgow with a counter-demonstration of their own.[36] This was preceded by a rally in Trafalgar Square on June 26 where Padmore, Chris Jones, James and F. A. Ridley all spoke about the Jamaican constitutional crisis.[37] The Glasgow demonstration was held on September 24 and 25. Padmore, though not a member, nevertheless was an ILP delegate, mainly because that party alone argued that in time of war it was the responsibility of colonial peoples to revolt against their distracted masters, a view favoured by many Indian Congress leaders and opposed by the communists at that time.[38] Munich and the threat of European war therefore meant manoeuvrability to colonial agitators. In September the IASB issued a manifesto entitled "Europe's Difficulty is Africa's Opportunity". They stressed that this was not a racist view, simply a realistic one. They were opposed to exploitation, not the colour of the exploiters' skin.[39]

Raymond Postgate, who at this time was editing an interesting journal of the left called *Fact*, asked Padmore to write something on Negro revolt, but he declined, being fully occupied with

IASB affairs.* A royal commission (under Lord Moyne) was about to investigate conditions in the West Indies, and the IASB, the LCP and the Negro Welfare Association (NWA) presented a joint petition. Padmore wrote it up for the *Defender*, where his former teacher, Dr Metz Lochard, now worked. Lochard offered him a job, and henceforth Padmore generally was identified as that paper's European correspondent.[40] Miss Cunard said that Padmore 'used to laugh much about their lamentable outlook', but was prepared to write the way the Negro press wanted.[41]

In November, Padmore again visited Germany, this time to report on growing colonialist sentiment in the Nazi state. He reported for the *Defender*[42] a huge rally at Berlin University and indicated how such affairs, widespread in Germany and viewed tolerantly abroad, raised apprehensions in colonial breasts.† On several occasions that year, he wrote about South African affairs, usually in the labour sphere, where he called for greater race awareness on the part of Africans. He also dwelt on the subject of the three High Commission Territories, whose transfer to South African control seemed likely. On the afternoon of May 8, for instance, the IASB organised a rally at Trafalgar Square to protest against such an occurrence, and Padmore described the 'colonial fascist' actions which were going on within the British empire while the world's attention was fixed upon other portions of the globe.[43]

---

* Postgate did get a most interesting alternative essay from C.L.R. James on "Negro Slave Revolts" (September 1938).

† Scholarly opinion is again veering to the conclusion that the Chamberlain government seriously considered attempting to satisfy Hitler with some African territory (see paper read by W. Roger Lewis at the African Studies Association meeting, Chicago, October 1964) but, even if this is exaggerated, here we are concerned with what Africans thought might happen. The editorial secretary of the IASB, William Harrison, a Negro American studying at the London School of Economics, wrote that growing race prejudice in Britain was disillusioning subject peoples, who more and more were inclined to discount British aims (see *Afro-American*, November 26, 1938). And the former editor of *WASU*, Ohenenana Cobina Kessie of Ashanti, produced a pamphlet "Colonies: What Africa Thinks", which went through two editions in a fortnight. He found white labour invariably racist, saw a European war as no concern of Africans and strongly criticised the reported hint that Nigeria might be transferred to the Germans in order to satisfy their African aspirations.

In January 1939 a conference partially sponsored by the IASB was held at Friends' House, Euston. Here socialists gathered from the Continent and the United Kingdom to discuss the popular front and warn colonial peoples of the danger which this tactic held for them. Padmore met a Frenchman named Daniel Guerin, who re-introduced him to the world of French colonialism. The contact was severed soon afterwards by political developments.[44] One positive result of the conference was the creation of a permanent Centre against Imperialism, a successor to the LAI minus the communists. The book dealer, Arthur Ballard, was important in this new body, which lasted till the Korean War, when it became the Movement for Colonial Freedom (MCF).

By April, according to the Special Branch, the IASB had encountered more internal troubles. Since Wallace-Johnson had returned to Sierra Leone, the secretaryship had passed into the hands of a Nigerian, Babalola Wilkey,* who ran into money troubles and left the IASB to form a Negro Cultural Association which affiliated to the eminently respectable National Council for Civil Liberties. In the meantime, the IASB moved from Gray's Inn Road to 12A Westbourne Grove and then, again without funds, to the offices of the ILP at 35 St Bride's. Padmore, in the view of the police—in this case a correct assumption—virtually ran ILP Negro affairs.[45] In June, Padmore published his views on military service. "Why I oppose conscription"[46] argued against supporting an imperialist war, against co-operating with capitalism, and declared that 'the enemy is at home!' His position was the orthodox one then; what differentiated him from most others of the ILP persuasion was his steadfastness in this view, as became apparent in the war years.

From July 7 to 9, a conference of coloured peoples met at Memorial Hall, Farringdon Street. The communists tried to control the proceedings, but Padmore, speaking as the representative both of the IASB and Wallace-Johnson's Sierra Leone Youth League, objected. It was a rough session and his dignity under fire impressed a young woman, who later, as the wife of the South African novelist Peter Abrahams, came to know Padmore well.[47] This restraint under attack was indicative of Padmore's attitude to

* During the war, Wilkey opened a Colonial Peoples' Club in Frith Street, Soho. See *LCP Newsletter*, No. 40, January 1943.

relations with the Communist Party. He was scornful of individual members, often ridiculing their tergiversation, duplicity and slavishness, but the party, as distinguished from its adherents, was another thing. He constantly recurred to Marxist theory and Russian practice of race relations and, because of this, would not condemn, especially in print, manifestly outrageous policies.

In the summer of 1939, European socialist parties met in Paris. Padmore attended, representing the Pan-African movement. Two good illustrations of his character are recalled by his ILP friend John McNair, who interpreted for the English-speaking contingent.

On the morning of the second day I saw him there. I asked him if he were properly fixed regarding 'digs' etc. He said he was quite OK and thanked me. A few minutes after, a good French socialist comrade, Marceau Pivert, who died three years ago, came up to me. He said, 'I see you have been chatting to George.' I answered, 'Yes, I was just enquiring about his lodgings.' Marceau then said, 'Do you know where he slept last night? At a dirty, down-and-out sixpenny doss-house.' I was alarmed and astonished. I was sleeping in a decent hotel in a room with two beds, one of which was waiting for Fenner Brockway who had not arrived. I went up to George during the morning and said, as I knew I should have to be very careful, 'Will you do me a favour, George?' 'Of course, John, anything I can do.' 'Listen', I said, 'I am compelled to sleep in a big double bedded room and I'm bored to death. There is an empty bed waiting for Fenner and he isn't coming. Will you come and share the room with me?' George hesitated a moment and then said, 'I haven't got much money, John.' I replied at once and told him that the room had been paid for by the ILP whether the spare bed was occupied or not. He then agreed to come. Next morning, when the maid brought in my French breakfast she saw George in the other bed and uttered a shriek. I laughed and said in French, 'Don't be silly, just go and get another breakfast for my friend.' This she did and George and I set to. After the meal I had some notes to make before Conference started and George said he would just take a stroll around. The time came when we should have to start for the Conference. I looked for George all over the hotel and couldn't find him. After enquiries I was directed to the kitchen where a black gentleman had been seen. I went there and there was old George at the sink, washing up the dishes, surrounded by three or four laughing French maids. I soon made short work of this and took him off protesting to the Conference.[48]

On the third day of the meeting, Padmore spoke. McNair, who translated into French, said that 'his English hearers were spellbound. When I translated his speech fully into French it brought the house down', for 'he had vision and imagination and his was the voice of the oppressed'. Padmore's theme was his usual one: the inevitability of decolonisation and the necessity for erecting a black bastion which at first would be capitalist-controlled, but ultimately socialist. In this task the British workers could help.[49]

In the last days before the war, the IASB issued its "Warning to the Coloured Peoples", a final statement that Nazis, fascists and democrats alike were imperialist bandits, that their conflict had no heroes or villains so far as oppressed colonial peoples were concerned.[50] Padmore reiterated his point in the war's first months, when he wrote that all popular leaders in the West Indies and Sierra Leone instantly had been imprisoned under emergency regulations 'for the duration'. Africans had received nothing from the victors of the first global conflict of the century, and there was no reason to believe they would fare any better in the aftermath of the second one. If France and Britain wished the support of their colonial captives, they should put their houses in order at once. Capitalist imperialism must give way to a world socialist federation, he said, recurring to one of his favourite themes of those years.[51]

4

'The Worst Racket Invented by Man': Padmore and the Empire at War

THE YEAR ENDED with Europe locked in the 'phoney war'. Prime Minister Chamberlain's latest utterance on the subject of imperialism allowed Padmore to finish 1939 with one of his most heated articles: "The British Empire is the Worst Racket yet Invented by Man".[1] He was incensed at Chamberlain's bland disclaimer that 'if imperialism means a certain racial superiority, suppression of political and economic freedom of other peoples, exploitation of resources of other countries for the benefit of the imperialist countries, then I say those are not characteristic of this country'. The effrontery staggered Padmore. As so often in the past, he urged British workers to stop their tacit support of the empire. Africans, he declared, do not want national freedom, except as a step towards world federation; and this will not be possible till capitalism and imperialism are finished. Several months later he startled a meeting of Federal Unionists at New Barnet by attacking imperialism and urging a form of federal socialism* for the devolved empire.[2] At this time, then, Padmore and the ILP were in agreement: 'We were against Hitler and all he stood for when he was being supported by the City of London and when British merchants were flooding Germany with the war goods and munitions he wanted. We were always against him and

* His later exclusive interest in Pan-Africanism was but a limitation upon his original aim. Nkrumah remains the principal exponent of these views in an apparently indifferent Africa.

58

any form of Totalitarianism and the best and only way to beat him and the Nazis was "to make Britain Socialist now".'[3] Padmore, of course, had the added distaste of the coloured colonial who finds himself involved in the white imperialists' wars.

Somewhat inconsistently, Padmore, though opposed to the war and resentful of black troops doing the white man's work, nevertheless joined others in demanding that the services drop their colour bar. Coloured Britons were not being called up and the many colonial blacks in the United Kingdom stood even less chance of entry into the forces. The IASB, WASU, the LCP and the Negro Welfare Association lobbied the various ministries and, on June 28, 1940, the Air Ministry announced that, for the duration, the RAF would accept coloured officer candidates. Babatunde Azakija, the son of a Nigerian politician, and the son and daughter of Dr Moody were the first selected.[4] The issue of coloured participation was not so easily settled, however; the LCP devoted an entire issue of their *Newsletter*[5] to Moody's correspondence with Lord Moyne, a year after a delegation had spoken to Moyne's predecessor as Secretary for the Colonies, Malcolm MacDonald, about recruitment of coloured men into the colonial service. Arthur Lewis, by now a junior lecturer at the LSE, summed up beautifully. It seems there was no colour bar, but if there were it could not be let down in wartime, etc. Unlike his friend Kenyatta, who went down to Sussex as a 'directed labour' farm-hand, Padmore refused even this minimal contribution to the war effort. In a letter which he tried out on his friend Dr Clarke, Padmore, in October 1943, told the Minister of Labour, Ernest Bevin, that he would refuse to accept any directed employment. Even though he could have gained exemption as a journalist, and indeed, according to his nephew, was offered a post in the Ministry of Information, he declined, preferring prison he said, rather than 'help in any way the war effort of British Imperialism or any other Imperialism'. Bevin for some reason decided to ignore this challenge; perhaps, Clarke later speculated, because Padmore was the one black the authorities were determined not to martyr.

During the early months of the war, Padmore and McNair spoke all over the south of England with 'the unwelcome support of the communists who then stated that we were engaged in a capitalist and Imperialist War.* This was their line until June 22, 1941, when Hitler invaded Russia. Then the war suddenly became a war for freedom and Democracy and they became our bitterest enemies. Their attacks were unscrupulous and they went all out for George because he was black.† He always remained calm and courteous and in any real debate he simply tore them to pieces.'[6] Later that lovely but desperate spring, the BBC, perhaps from a Dunkirk-induced sense of loneliness, re-examined its vocabulary at Padmore's urging. On May 11, one of its programme announcers repeatedly used the word 'nigger'. This time, however, the Corporation apologised when the IASB and the LCP complained. Padmore wrote hotly that it was 'incredible that the representative of ostensible "trustees" should speak so contemptibly of their ostensible "wards" '.[7] The word was banned from the air, though a year later Reginald Sorenson, MP, voiced the same complaint in the House of Commons.[8] The incident seemed to draw Padmore closer to the LCP for a while, for in the same month he spoke at their annual general meeting.[9]

The most important African news of the year came from French Equatorial Africa where the Governor General, Félix Eboué, a Negro from Guyane, decided to collaborate with de Gaulle and the London French, and defected from the Vichy French Governor General at Dakar. Padmore pointed out that Eboué probably acted not so much for de Gaulle as against Pétain's racist regime. The failure of the Anglo-French Dakar raid merely proved that de Gaulle should have recruited Senegalese to his cause. Padmore's old friend, Emile Faure, the Senegalese President of the Ligue de Défense de la Race Nègre, whom the Daladier government had sent out of the metropole shortly after the war began, was an obvious contact, he wrote.[10]

The Lend-Lease destroyer bases deal also agitated Padmore, who pointed out that no one had bothered to listen to West Indian

---

* For an interesting analysis of the communist position, see the *New Statesman*, April 27, 1940; Strachey and Gollancz wrote that the communists felt that Britain and France were the aggressors, because they feared that, if Hitler were defeated, the western duo would be encouraged to attack Russia. Seen in this light, the strange little war in Finland looked much more ominous.

† Or because he was an ex-Comintern official?

protests at the possible extension of the American colour bar to the islands, and he applauded the Declaration of Rights which the West Indies National Council issued in Havana during the Pan-American Conference. He noted that, despite the objections of the United States Secretary of State, Cordell Hull, the concept of West Indian self-determination had been incorporated into the Act of Havana.[11] Padmore distinguished between freedom and national independence, in the West Indies as in Africa: 'We demand full self-determination not as an end in itself—for we are not narrow nationalists—but as the historic prerequisite for the free and voluntary co-operation between all nations and peoples and races.'[12]

Even without this stress on island affairs, Padmore was in no danger of being forgotten at home. During the three or four months of the winter 1940–41 when she was waiting in Trinidad while trying to get a passage to England, Nancy Cunard constantly met people who had copies of her banned book and others which contained Padmore essays. 'To the white authorities Padmore was anathema. . . . Despite his having been so long out of Trinidad, his name was revered, his work known.'[13] Miss Cunard was on her way back from Chile to England on the final leg of that trip to the Spanish Civil War front which had begun with Padmore over four years earlier. The authorities were most dubious about her presence in the island; the police—according to her own account—wished to detain her, despite the fact that her cousin, Sir Edward Cunard, was then an official in Port of Spain. A Negro policeman told her he had been informed but not convinced that her banned *Negro Anthology* was produced with 'Moscow gold', a commodity which the Colonial Police apparently believed in.[14] Wherever she went, she found evidence that even if Padmore's writings were proscribed, nevertheless people were familiar with them.

Early in 1941, Padmore described what the colonial press was saying about the war. According to his analysis of the *Gold Coast Spectator*, the *People* of Trinidad and Zik's Nigerian papers, colonial editors were impatient to learn of British war aims, especially as they affected the colonies. Colonials, he wrote, knew fascism at first hand and needed no instruction on that topic. They also knew that the present war was an imperialist one.[15] The case of Ethiopia was instructive: though the Emperor's state was freed of Italian control, the British government was remarkably silent about the postwar position. Moreover, there were hints, such as that in the *Daily Telegraph* of February 5, that South Africa probably would help Britain in making troop dispositions there. This sounded rather like South West Africa in the First World War. Padmore supposed Britain would try to control Ethiopia economically, if not politically.[16]

In July, he again attacked the Parliamentary Labour Party members of the wartime Coalition government, when he wrote about the arrest of Wilfred A. Domingo, long-time Harlemite and president of the West Indies National Council, who had returned to Kingston to contest a seat under the new constitution. By ignoring this high-handed behaviour on the part of the colonial government, the Labour Party men, in Padmore's opinion, rightly earned the contempt of colonial workers. Domingo's arrest was the cause of great dissatisfaction in Harlem and indirectly led to a question being asked in parliament, which George Hall, the (Labour) Under-Secretary of State for the Colonies, answered most feebly.[17] In a later article, "Jamaica Rejects Sham 'Democratic' Constitution", Padmore expertly discussed the history and present status of a polity in which the planter aristocracy could no longer take for granted its ability to perpetuate white supremacy under Crown rule.[18] The island was heading towards a Ceylonese sort of constitutional reform, he thought, though his Ceylonese anti-colonialist friends did not find this reassuring.

On August 8, Padmore again lectured to the ILP Summer School students, at University College, Bangor. He had had his tonsils removed, and his voice had acquired a husky quality which increased considerably when he spoke at length or was tired.[19] This time he spoke on "A Negro Looks at the War".[20] Throughout the year, a bad one for Londoners, he kept steadily at his political work, which among other things took him daily to the Ministry of Information, where he collected all the colonial news that he could, both for his own researches and for his dispatches to the Negro press in America. At year's end, Padmore summarised the Negro view of Europe's plight, saying clearly what some sectors of the Negro press occasionally hinted at: Europe had contrived its own downfall. The Germans were but Europeans writ large, doing in Europe what hitherto had been done outside that continent. Even indirect rule was practised by the Nazis: their chiefs and emirs were called Quislings. Curiously, Europeans could not see that the epithet applied outside Norway.[21]

Early in 1942, the matter of the Atlantic Charter and its applicability to colonies exercised Padmore. Shortly after the Churchill–Roosevelt talks at sea, Deputy Prime Minister Attlee had implied in the House of Commons that the Prime Minister and the President had spoken for all mankind. The Labour Party's *Daily Herald* promoted this interpretation under the heading "The Atlantic Charter—it Means Darker Races". And then, on September 9, Churchill, with characteristic Edwardian brutality, punctured the balloon. Azikiwe's *West African Pilot*, along with the Burmese and Indian press, retorted angrily. As Padmore saw it, the colonial powers were far more interested in preserving their positions in Asia than in fighting Japanese fascism.[22] Even the so-called anti-colonial forces within the Labour Party failed to understand the dynamic of historical process; as with Rita Hinden and other Fabian intellectuals, they refused to accept the 'Leninist, this only solution of the colonial problem, the single solution . . . which was largely responsible for securing the one worth-while achievement of the twentieth century to date—the October Revolution'.[23] Azikiwe, who earlier (August 16) had cabled Churchill: 'Are we fighting [the word was used with licence] for the security of Europe to enjoy the Four Freedoms whilst West Africans* continue to live under pre-war status?', again cabled his discontent, and asked Padmore 'to interview the Prime Minister on the matter on his return from America'.[24] The interview never came off. So far as Britain was concerned—America was another matter—the subject was closed in March when Under-Secretary Harold Macmillan made it quite clear to a fellow parliamentarian, R. Sorenson, that the government had no intention of applying the 'relevant clauses of the Atlantic Charter'. Indeed, it would be a work of supererogation to do so, as this was precisely the point of the British empire: to bring subject peoples to self-rule and independence under the Crown.[25] In his account of this exchange in the House, Padmore made good use of a work from the enemy's camp, Professor

* The regional exclusiveness should be noted.

Margery Perham's *Africans and British Rule*, which was quite specific on African dislike of the Northern Nigerian or Lugard system of indirect rule.

Though they had been rebuffed in proper Churchillian fashion, West African students refused to accept that Allied war aims had nothing to do with them. In this conviction they naturally had Padmore's full support. In the summer of 1942, WASU organised its second conference on West Africa with the theme of democracy and its application to the region. Speakers demanded internal responsibility now and the democratisation of district and village councils, all to be built upon the existing base of African communalism. They were unimpressed with official claims that conditions were too varied in the four territories to allow them to be treated in one legislative instrument. They dismissed as platitudinous Creech Jones and Sorenson, the two most vocally anti-colonial Labour MPs, and they were impressed with Russian achievements among illiterate peasants. Their lengthy resolutions on economic, land tenurial, social and educational problems were joined to one which reaffirmed their decision of April 4, 1942, that internal self-government now and freedom within five years was their minimum demand.[26] Though he approved, Padmore clearly regarded this generation of African students as but a prelude to freedom. Earlier, concerning representations made by WASU to the Colonial Secretary, Padmore had written: 'Personally, I welcome the forward step which the students have taken, for it must not be forgotten that the majority of Colonial students in Britain are from the upper and middle classes—the sons and daughters of the native bourgeoisie, professional men, Government officials, chiefs and other petty rulers.' This memo, considering the petitioners' social circumstances, showed the positive influence of anti-colonial agitation, however, and Padmore hoped that after fascism's defeat a socialist Africa might co-operate with a federated, socialist Britain and Europe.[27]

Finally back in London, Nancy Cunard took up her friendship with Padmore again, seeing Dorothy Pizer (whom she had not known before) and him sporadically. These three people usually met either at the Padmore apartment in North London or in a public house in Tottenham Court Road, "The Horseshoe", one of the pubs where racial conflict, which had increased considerably with the advent of American troops, was improbable. Padmore, who at this time spent his days at the Ministry of Information Press Office, would appear 'with stacks of paper under his arm, exhausted, but valiant'. He seemed untouched personally by the heightened tension, apparently able to live above the cruel contradiction which racism offered in the 'struggle for democracy'. Miss Cunard remembered interviewing at this time coloured servicemen, to write a series of propaganda pieces for the Ministry of Information. One in particular, a much-decorated Trinidadian named Jimmy Hyde, stuck in her mind. ' "No friend, no girl, no one in all England", said he; "I am alone and the only time I feel at all happy is when I am in my Spitfire alone in the clouds." We had to wait about 40 minutes to have dinner in the ordinary hotel at Ashford, near London, till the white officers and airmen had left the dining room.'* To tell Padmore 'a thing like this was to evoke that well-known, light laughter of his. I can hear it yet.'[28]

In the next year Padmore and she collaborated on a pamphlet of some consequence, *The White Man's Duty*, which resulted from Dorothy Pizer's severely edited transcript of several conversations that spring. They took as their theme the various declarations, centring on Roosevelt's pronouncement of the 'four freedoms', and applied them to the British empire. It sold well.

When news of the fall of Singapore reached London, Padmore told F. A. Ridley that it signified the end of the white man's imperium. The decision to accept coloured men in the British forces had been dictated by necessity; unfortunately for the British, there were few colonials sufficiently educated to be of much service. As he had noted earlier: 'Imperialism, like Nazism,

---

* The advent of American troops naturally exacerbated this situation. One of the more startling cases of American racism known to the British public was that of Corporal Leroy Henry, a Negro American soldier, who, on the flimsiest of evidence—an English prostitute's testimony— was convicted of rape and sentenced to death. George Orwell exposed the affair in the *Tribune*, representations were made, letters appeared in the press and, in June 1944, when he might have been expected to show preoccupation with larger issues, General Eisenhower reprieved the luckless soldier (see the *Defender*, July 1, 1944, which displayed an interesting fascination with the sexual exploits of Negro Americans in England). The virulence of American racism surprised the British, who were used to a more genteel expression of the same attitude.

is a system that cannot afford to educate its victims.'[29] The British were now reaping what they had sowed but not bargained for. In the July 1942 issue of *The Crisis*, Padmore underlined the point. The Singapore disaster was not surprising, for how were a people to 'assume responsibility in defence of the system which until then had failed to recognize their existence?' If only the British could understand the benefits of decolonisation, Padmore told Miss Cunard:

> The relationship between the indigenous populations and the army in India, and the scattered forces in the Colonies at present occupied in policing those regions against revolt and civil disturbance would undergo a complete change. These forces would no longer be regarded as the instruments of alien operations, but rather as friends and allies. A comparison: the Australians have welcomed the American contingents who have reached their shores. In this changed atmosphere the vast man-power of India could be drawn upon. Industrial and agricultural resources would be exploited in a new burst of energy having behind it the full force of political movements which are today operating against England. The world would be electrified by a change of policy which would turn the slogan of 'Democracy' into a living reality—into the struggle of free peoples, regardless of race, for their common rights against a menace felt equally by all. Thereby also would be nullified the activities of Nazi and Fifth Column agents. Do not forget: Rome abandoned her Colonies to save herself, losing both herself and her Colonies. Yet Britain, by freeing her Colonies, can save both herself and them and lay the foundations of a new Commonwealth of Nations, bound together in equal partnership.[30]

The sentiments were generous, unrelated to Marxist theory, affected by Padmore's Russian experience (of which more later) and in keeping with the 'one worldism' so fashionable that year.

In 1943 Padmore brought out a series of essays in the *New Leader*, in which he again stigmatised indirect rule as a fraud, a variant on fascist administrative technique which used black Quislings to collect taxes and maintain order.[31] Even the new approach, signalled by the 1940 creation of a Colonial Development and Welfare Fund in response to the serious flaws in colonial rule brought to light in the Moyne Report on the West Indies, was a hoax. Nothing but a new series of research committees had come of this, most of the Moyne recommendations had been shelved for the duration, the great corporations continued to dominate colonial economies and exact huge wartime profits, and the indications were, Padmore wrote, that the postwar world would be a fine one for capitalists.* When the 'Beveridge Plan' for social security in Britain had been set aside by the coalition government, he added, colonials understandably were cynical about their own chances. 'When the ruling class of Britain won't give "Beveridge" to the people at home, how can they be expected to give rice and curry to the natives abroad?'[32]

Such reforms as did arise out of Royal Commission recommendations he usually saw as blinds, as devices for the continuation of colonial rule by other means. This led him to make certain errors of judgement, as in the case of the Trade Union Labour Officers, those trade unionists recommended for secondment to the colonial governments by Major G. St J. Orde Browne shortly before the war.[33] Padmore presumed that they would be in charge of unions and necessarily subordinate to conventional Colonial Office superiors, whereas in practice, at least in Northern Rhodesia, this was not the case. He was justified, though, in being critical of the pose adopted by the British representatives at the International Labour Organisation conference in New York during October 1941. Only a casuist could maintain that the Colonial Office was fostering colonial trade unionism. True, papers had been written to that effect, and conditions varied greatly from colony to colony, but it was too much to claim that general policy aimed at this goal. One indication was that no coloured representative attended the conference, nor did anyone seem surprised. In any case, the British would have been hard put to find any trade unionists, had they wanted to, as most were languishing in British jails. Men such as

* In 1940 he had been especially exercised over the government's handling of strikes and rioting in the Northern Rhodesian Copperbelt. Padmore first covered this dramatic and bloody affair in an article for the *New Leader*, April 18, 1940: "We gave them copper—they gave us lead"; he followed this up in the December 7 issue with "Lloyd suppresses another Report", charging that the Colonial Office was allowing the copper companies to make huge wartime profits in a conscious arrangement with white labour and local government at the expense of the black miners.

Bustamante, Wallace-Johnson and Uriah Butler could have added to the proceedings, but not in any decorous, tasteful fashion.[34]

Padmore expanded his disillusionment in an article, "Blue Print of Post-War Anglo-American Imperialism", which appeared in *Left*, October 1943. By this time he and Jon Evans were the joint editors of this organ of the ILP. C. A. Smith, who had edited it since its inception under the title *Controversy* in August 1936, resigned in May 1942 after falling out with Brockway and others over pacifism's relationship to socialism. In his essay, Padmore argued that, without an empire, Britain would be reduced to a small, rather poor and powerless island. Obviously, neither of the two major political parties was going to consent to this, especially as it would mean a transfer of power to the Americans first of all. As with Britain a century ago, so today the United States, because of its strength, called for one world, a free trade globe in which it had no competition. The British tried to answer this in the plan, which Field Marshal Jan Smuts drafted, for the creation of regions of special influence: for example, East, Central and Southern Africa for the British. In such a sphere, the British might safely invite American capital participation. By such means—and a speech which Lord Hailey made to the Royal Central Asian Society on August 7 seemed to support Padmore—the entire non-Russian world could be shared out. Even the Fabians, Padmore suggested, were coming to the same conclusions. As he had rejected the Comintern idea of a Pan-Africa, so he also declined to accept the Smuts version.[35]

The August visit to the United Kingdom of eight West African newspapermen (three Nigerians, the most important being Nnamdi Azikiwe, two Gold Coasters, two Sierra Leoneans and a Gambian), at the invitation of the British Council, confirmed Padmore's cynical view. They were brought to Britain to learn of the sacrifices being made by the imperial government and the English people, and thus acquire a new perspective on the war. This hope was not fulfilled. The eight, instead of concluding that they had a stake in the war, recurred to the subject of colonial democracy, issuing a memo entitled "The Atlantic Charter and British West Africa". In it they called for the abrogation of the Crown colony system and the immediate institution of representative government, to be followed after a decade by five years of responsible (i.e. internally independent) government, and then dominion status. Their embarrassing return to a subject already settled (at least to his satisfaction) by Churchill received no notice in the British press, though, as Padmore remarked, lots of photos of these men in their colourful native garb appeared in certain papers.[36] Even the *Anti-Slavery Reporter*, hardly a severe critic of African aspirations, doubted their aims could be reached in anything so short as ten years.[37]

5

Anti-Stalinist Defends the Soviet Union

IT WAS NOTED by *WASU* writers that the Russians had done
something qualitatively different in the mass education of the
peoples of their Asian republics. This matter of Russia and
colonialism is so important and so fundamental to an understanding of Padmore that the subject must be considered at length.
Soon after Dunkirk, Padmore wrote an article entitled "To Defeat
Nazism We Must Free Colonials". Liberals, he declared, who
decide that some colonies, such as India, are ready for freedom,
while others, such as the African ones, are not, themselves use a
Hitlerian approach. Who gave them the right to judge the progress
made by men of other colours?[1] He returned to this attack upon
liberal attitudes two years later when he wrote that Norman Leys
and Rita Hinden (whose *Colour Bar in East Africa* and *Plan for
Africa*, respectively, he was reviewing) made an identical mistake.
Both deplored the iniquities of empire without realising (or ad-
mitting) that only one state, Russia under the Soviets, had solved
the problem.[2] From this time he began developing in the pages of
the *New Leader* the ideas that ultimately appeared in his book
(written in collaboration with Dorothy Pizer) *How Russia Transformed her Colonial Empire: A Challenge to Imperialist Powers*. To a
great extent, he was influenced by the prevailing sense of admiration for the fighting qualities of Britain's eastern ally. In a period
when Hollywood turned out films about those four great de-
mocracies (Britain, China, the United States and the Soviet Union,
for those with an insecure grasp upon recent history), Padmore was
a participant in the general mood. As his admirer Subasinghe puts
it: 'He often pointed out that a multi-national state like the Soviet

Union could and would maintain its solidarity and hold out against a powerful enemy mainly because of the gains of the people and the manner in which the national question had been solved. This view and his supreme confidence were justified as subsequent events showed.'[3]

Though his views on colonialism were avowedly Leninist, Padmore was fond of pointing out the pedigree of Lenin's ideas. 'In arriving at his conclusions, Lenin drew much of his data from the distinguished Liberal, J. A. Hobson's famous study on Imperialism, which was first published in 1902.'[4] In a footnote to this, he went on: 'The three writers who have had the greatest influence upon the author's political views on Colonialism are J. A. Hobson, Nikolai Lenin and Professor Thomas Parker Moon, whose *Imperialism and World Politics* still remains a constant source of reference. The first of these was an Englishman, the second a Russian and the third an American.'

In the spring of 1943, he noted that the loss of European Russia had not signified the end of the state, because the eastern regions had been industrialised. This task had been much harder than that facing the British in India or Africa because the transition from feudal to modern industrial conditions had been effected without passage through the intermediate capitalist stage. However, it had led to enormous gains in the first Five Year Plan period, leading even to a transformation in agriculture. 'Co-operation between the various races and peoples is the new note in the Soviet East.'[5] As he put it a little earlier in *The Crisis*, the Soviet Union 'has done more to liquidate illiteracy and raise the cultural level of the former subject races of Central Asia within twenty-five years, than the British Government has accomplished in India or Africa in two centuries'.[6] The disappearance of the capitalist–imperialist Russian regime meant the disappearance of the 'oppressor–oppressed relationship between the imperialist metropolis and the colonial periphery', which the Germans were learning at great cost.[7]

The lengthiest exposition of this thesis written by Padmore before his book appeared, was an article called "Russia Destroyed her Empire!" which George Orwell published in *Tribune*, February 12, 1943. 'Without a doubt', Padmore asserted, 'Soviet unity in resisting the invader is due to the policy of self-determination which the Soviet Government undertook in relation to the national minorities and communities which before 1917 formed what might be called the colonial territories of the Czarist Empire.' It was the custom of nineteenth-century empires to insist upon the use of the ruling language, a policy which backfired with the growth of a sense of national grievance in the Austro-Hungarian and Russian territories. Wherever the subject peoples could, they developed bodies of vernacular literature. So, too, after 1917, the same thing occurred in the regions of eastern Russia where, however, the Soviet state itself provided education in the local tongues. This course was adopted only after Lenin had won over his critics in inner party circles who favoured the adoption of Great Russian and whom he accused of latent chauvinism and of continuing czarist practice. 'In my view', Lenin had remarked, 'a Communist who thinks in this way is a pan-Russian jingo.' Padmore admitted that it was difficult to use local languages on the secondary level and practically impossible at universities and technical colleges, but argued that to learn Russian as a second language was to acquire a means of participating in the world's wider cultural opportunities. Especially was this true for Muslim women, who experienced a class, national and sex liberation at the hands of bolshevik missionaries in Central Asia. Whereas socialism unites, Padmore found that:

> Imperialism divides. Under Imperialism, the native races of Asia and Africa are being kept as illiterate as possible, for history shows that as soon as an educated minority emerges among such a subject people it becomes the voice of the national aspirations of the backward inarticulate masses. The idea of national and cultural independence and political unity among multi-racial and national groups is possible only along the lines of a socialised planned economy. And that is why we are witnessing today the tremendously heroic stand of a multi-national State (which, because of its many, many different peoples, cannot be called 'Russian') which is the marvel of the whole world.[8]

However, his friend John McNair remembers that in debates with communists during the war Padmore used to claim that the 'Russian Communists were the worst of all Imperialists in their subversion of the Baltic Provinces, their attack on Finland and their record in Poland'.[9] My impression is that once he had written a manuscript, he could not bear to have it overtaken by events. Moreover, he was never one to supply the anti-communists with ammunition; witness his insistence that only socialists had the right to condemn Stalin for doing in Finland what the imperialists always do everywhere: 'We must, while repudiating Stalin's Finnish adventure, dissociate ourselves from all entanglements with the imperialist warmongers and their anti-Soviet campaign.'[10] 'He distrusted Russian Communist leadership', a Swedish friend later wrote, 'and held to socialist goals only when the majority was prepared to vote for them. He saw through Stalin as a harsh tyrant.'[11] Later in the war, his thesis seemed to be contradicted in Eastern Europe.

One other book which curiously complemented Padmore's was written at the same time by his acquaintance, Leonard Barnes, who in 1944 produced *Soviet Light on the Colonies*, an imaginary dialogue between a British traveller and his Russian guest, who attempted to compare Soviet experience in Asia with that of the British in the Rhodesias. Though Barnes and Padmore had met at least as early as 1935, when they appeared at the same conference, they seem never to have been close, and there is no evidence that Padmore took Barnes's book into consideration when writing his own. *Soviet Light* is a far better work, gracefully written, subtle and full of examples. That two such books could be written at about the same time suggests the impact which Soviet Russia made in left circles during the war, in effect erasing the bad marks earned during the purges and in Finland and Poland.

What, then, was Padmore's book about? Briefly, nothing which he had not written before. By way of establishing his credentials, he mentioned (in a preface written in June 1945) that he had been in Russia for three years and never encountered the 'slightest manifestation of racial chauvinism or colour bar', and that he had been on the Moscow Soviet, though he could not have aspired to the Port of Spain City Council. Moreover, he added, whatever else may be said against Stalin, he generally followed Lenin's view of the right of self-determination for national minorities. Both utterances formed the canvas upon which he projected his view, first announced in this form in 1943, that 'Imperialism divides; Socialism unites'. Looking at the defenders of Russia, Padmore found them polyglot and multi-racial, in contrast with those who (willingly) defended the western regimes. With the exception of the Filipinos, who had been promised freedom from the Americans by 1946, Asians had been apathetic to Allied losses in 1942. The Red Army was an instrument of education, of social change. In Russia, the formerly despised Jews, the inhabitants of czarist ghettos, had a role: over one hundred of them were general officers in 1944. All of this had come about because of Lenin's insistence upon the right of self-determination, which was not to be confused with the Wilsonian theme of capitalist national exclusivity. Still, one must not conclude that all was well in the Soviet Union. 'There are certain shortcomings in the Soviet Regime, especially the curtailment of workers' democracy', which came about because the revolution succeeded only in a poor and backward state surrounded by powerful enemies. However, the consolidation of power would bring forth a new liberalism; in the meantime, socialists must work both to aid the motherland of their creed and to promote change in their own countries.

His manuscript started life as a commissioned work for Gollancz's Left Book Club which, by this time, had wearied of pursuing the labyrinthine party line. Padmore's argument that there was little to choose between Allied and Nazi imperialisms offended Gollancz, who compensated Padmore but refused to accept the book. The author then took it to a young man he had met early in 1944, Dennis Dobson, who was teaching in the city of Cambridge and trying to establish a press. Padmore's book interested Dobson, who requested a reader's opinion from the Sovietologist, Walter Kolarz.

Though Kolarz had doubts about Padmore's familiarity with Russian history, and did not believe that the Central Asian peoples were more backward under the czars than were any African peoples, he was in the main favourably inclined. Czarist statistics used by Soviet scholars were very misleading, revealing altogether too great a disparity between the literacy accomplishments of the two regimes, according to Kolarz, and he felt Padmore should have mentioned the disappearance of the German Volga Republic. However, he agreed that 'colour bar is contrary to the mentality of the Russian peoples and not only to the official policy'. After various strictures relating to industrial production, railway trackage and historical interpretation, Kolarz wrote:

I have a great deal of sympathy with the cause which the author is advocating. This cause is very seldom put forward in book form and it most certainly deserves to be. The value of the book lays [sic] much more in the cause for which it fights than in the material which it contains on the USSR since there are many books dealing with Soviet policy on nationalities (and containing similar material) but only very few link up this policy with the problem of the coloured peoples in general. It is rather fortunate that the author does not stick rigidly to the subject which the title indicates but that he quite often deviates to the general aspects of the Negro problem, to the situation of the colonial peoples in other countries, etc. I think the book would gain in value if this part of it was even more elaborated. I would even suggest that a subtitle should be added, stressing this particular angle of the book.

Dobson showed Kolarz's report to Padmore, who was stung. 'Rubbish', he wrote across it, 'how these people hate Lenin!' And a little later he wrote *ad hominem* that Kolarz turned out 'just the sort of stuff that English intellectuals love'. 'The man is a typical Central European social-democrat, the sort who can tell you all about revolutions but never attempt making one.'[12] This was cruel, and years later came home when his sometime close friend, the South African novelist Peter Abrahams, travestied Padmore in a similar fashion in his novel *A Wreath for Udomo*. Nevertheless, Padmore later took some of Kolarz's suggestions: for example, he got his hundred Jewish generals and the book's subtitle from Dobson's reader.

Padmore feared a break in the Allied front and a western war with Russia. Kolarz would come in handy then, but his own work would be unmarketable. 'It's difficult for an honest man to write in a period of rabid nationalism and jingoistic imperialism. Do let me hear from you', he wrote to Dobson in April, 'as I think the whole question of empire and socialism is going to be one of the big issues brought home to the British people in the near future.'[13] He was persuaded that the experience of a wartime Coalition cabinet showed that Tory and Labour members alike would create a reactionary united front as soon as Hitler was destroyed, and that this would mean the worst for colonial peoples, whose aspirations would be denounced as 'communist'. (Here he was on firmer ground.)

In July, with the manuscript finally corrected, Padmore again wrote to Dobson about the Kolarz review, which obviously worried him. 'Excuse this long letter,* it was written only because there is a raid on and I am sitting in the Underground waiting for the "All Clear" and thought it useful to pass the time away in this manner. So you must blame Adolf for causing me to inflict this long epistle on you.' Padmore's fundamental problem was to destroy Kolarz's assertion that historical continuity characterised Russian developments. He did not say clearly enough for Kolarz that Russians always had looked at others in a way 'very different from that of other great white nations towards the colonial peoples'. Such an admission would have been fatal to Padmore's thesis, and he resisted. 'Compelled to face realities, they fall back upon "Holy Russia" and the dear old "Russian Soul" ', he jotted scornfully. 'Quite true, every great social change carries over certain permanent features of the past—language, ethnic composition, fauna, flora, topography, etc. etc., but Revolutions upset the social, economic, and political arrangement between *social classes* and in the case of the Russian Revolution, between the racial and national elements making up the old Russian Czarist Empire. That is the main thesis of my book.' How Kolarz, who 'obviously belongs to that coterie of Central European Social Democratic liberals who have suddenly "discovered" the USSR but don't like the *fundamental* achievements of the glorious October Revolution', could believe that 'the USSR is just the same old Russia' baffled Padmore. Still, Kolarz knew what the 'superficial British public' wanted and gave 'them a full dose of their own prejudices' in *Stalin and Eternal Russia* (published in 1944).[14]

The V-2 attacks had begun to sap Britain's morale by late June, when Padmore wrote that he hoped to get out of London for some sleep the coming weekend. 'I am so tired', he said the next month, 'that I have very little energy to do more than is absolutely necessary these days. . . . I am anxious to see the proof sheets before Hitler

---

* An idiosyncrasy noted by all his friends was his civilised distaste for the telephone. 'I hate telephones and won't have one in my flat', he wrote, in a letter to Daniel Guerin, a decade later (October 15, 1954).

starts sending over his v-3. It's no joke.'[15] A few days later, on July 30, 1944, he wrote to Dobson again to advise him 'that in the event of anything happening to me I want you to get in touch with my friend and executor Mr Joseph de Silva of 8 Belsize Lane [London] NW3 who has full authority to look after my affairs. The MS must be published as it stands. There must be no changes. Arthur Ballard's shop was destroyed on Friday. Poor fellow! One lives from day to day and must prepare for the worst.' Dobson acknowledged the message, but trusted that he would not 'have to have any dealings with Mr de Silva'. This, for those interested in things military, contrasts sharply with Padmore's absolute silence on the 1940–41 raids by Luftwaffe planes. Padmore was not too preoccupied with his own neck to stop performing his usual acts of kindness. 'I remember the great pains he took to save the life of an old West Indian seafaring friend of his (I believe his name was Chrys Jones) who was living in poor circumstances in the East End of London', writes Ambassador Subasinghe. 'He was deeply moved and stricken with grief upon his death.'[16] Jones, Nancy Cunard's platform associate, had named his last child Reginald George after Reynolds and Padmore,[17] and Padmore always felt a special responsibility for the family of this tough, cheerful, uneducated worker.[18]

Book production in war conditions is a very difficult matter. Paper is hard to come by, book agents' shops are blown up, labour and machinery are committed elsewhere, and transport is irregular. Padmore faced all these problems. By mid-summer 1944, he was anxious to get his book off his hands and started on another. He had persuaded the International African Service Bureau to let him have some decent paper from its own stock, but delay followed delay, time dragged on and in 1945 the proof sheets were still incomplete. Padmore again had cut the manuscript, but could not alter his 'fundamental political arguments for history is already underlining the correctness of my thesis', he remarked in October. By January 1946, Dorothy Pizer had done so much work on the book,* which

---

* Though she herself rarely appeared in print, she was capable of writing sensibly. See her article on the Liberian centenary in *Socialist Leader*, August 16, 1947, a brief, straightforward potted history which leaves out conflicts with Garvey and the League of Nations, hails Tubman's new era and, surprisingly, is not anti-Firestone.

Padmore was 'completely sick' of, that he told Dobson to add her name to the title page as co-author.[19]

When the book did appear in September 1946, the left was indignant. C. A. Smith, who at this time was editing *Common Wealth Review*, the organ of Sir Richard Acland's social justice and pro-war party, thought the book disgraceful. He gave it to a young trade unionist and rising political figure, Walter Padley (today an MP and member of the Wilson government) for review, setting in train a lengthy series of acrimonious articles and replies. Smith remembers that Padmore wrote to him privately, not challenging the facts which Padley brought out, but protesting against the unfair spirit of his review. Padmore and Smith, who had known each other for a decade, never met again. Peter Abrahams next broke into print with an attack upon Padley. The argument centred on Padmore's contention that Russia had decolonised and Padley's reply that postwar Eastern Europe disproved this. In their exchanges, Padley remarked to Abrahams that Padmore, of all men, knew what communist cynicism could be. To quote Lenin's "Declaration of the Rights of Subject Peoples" was not enough. One had to consider what really transpires in the Soviet republics, one had an obligation to recall the Volga Germans, one had to look at Eastern Europe today. They rejoined and rebutted in the issues of January 25 and February 1, 1947, and then the paper's columns were closed to this discussion. From that time may be dated the start of Padmore's estrangement from the ILP and the world of the British left. He usually spoke harshly of Padley henceforth. They last met at Lord's during the visit of the Australian cricketers in 1948.

Padley did not reciprocate this coolness. He thought Padmore 'the biggest Negro I've ever known, intellectually and in character'.[20] On several occasions during the war, he had urged Padmore to stand for parliament as an ILP or ILP-supported Independent, which is certainly an indication of his trust in the man, and he regarded the West Indian as a leading light of the party for the decade 1936–47. Padley had the final word, though, for his own book *Soviet Russia: Free Union or Empire?* (published in Bombay in 1947, with an introduction by Jayaprakesh Narayan and a preface by Fenner Brockway) holds Padmore up for inspection as a typical product of socialist fuzziness on the subject of Soviet imperialism. A totalitarian empire such as this, Padley observed, was no model for those who sought to liquidate western imperialism. The American, Dwight MacDonald, who had printed Padmore's work from May 1944, published much of Padley's book in the Spring 1948 issue of his own magazine, *Politics*, and there the matter rested.

Misgivings also were expressed by the older generation of African nationalists, such as Dr J. B. Danquah. In an autobiographical note which he drafted while under arrest at the Lisbon Hotel Annex in Accra Airport on April 9, 1948, he said that Padmore's book had interested him, though when he had checked Padmore's statistics relating to the war debt Britain owed the Gold Coast, he had found them inaccurate.[21]

The work did not sell. Review copies were sent off to twenty-seven British, twenty-four African, twenty West Indian and eight American periodicals, newspapers and research organisations without much effect. Padmore's own fears had been realised: 'If you don't hurry up the book', he had chided Dobson early in 1945, 'it will be dated not so much by its contents but by events in Europe. For it will have no public when the clash comes with the su as things indicate.'[22] He was right, for when he tried to find an American publisher—John Day had been mentioned—it was too late. Three of them found the book 'completely pro-Soviet'. They were wrong to credit Padmore with being a Russian propagandist but, without knowing the man or the date when he wrote his book, could be forgiven for this assumption. It was a book which depended on a few clearly-stated and deeply-felt beliefs. That these views led him to occasional intemperate outbursts and to a rupture of several friendships was unfortunate but understandable. As Padmore remarked to Dobson: 'Once I commit myself to a point of view, I defend it until I am convinced that I am wrong', which was one reason why he liked the ponderous but clear and tenacious writings of Stalin.[23] But, by 1947, readers in the West were not much interested in distinctions, and his work suffered accordingly. It was ignored, except in the leftwing press, and there it fared badly, an early victim of the cold war.

6

The Road to Manchester

THE ONLY HOPE for world peace, Padmore argued, was the
establishment of truly socialist regimes after the destruction of
Hitler's armies. 'How I would like to see a real British Socialist
Common Wealth Federation—white and coloured', he wrote to
Dobson in October 1944. But he held little hope for this outcome.
Existing organisations were not socialist: even the ILP lacked a
revolutionary basis, though men such as Brockway did not seem to
recognise it. The clash between Ernest Bevin and Aneurin Bevan
was symptomatic of the quarrels one expected between actual
socialists and the trade union capitalists who dominated the
Parliamentary Labour Party. Several generations earlier, Engels
had warned Kautsky about the progressive bourgeoisification of
the British working class, and his admonition still appeared
germane. Perhaps there was time to build the New Jerusalem, but
the recent love affair between the Colonial Office and the trades
unions suggested that it was nearly over.[1]

Paul Robeson said in 1944 that 'the United States will have a
tremendous lot to say about what happens in Africa after the
war'.[2] Padmore was convinced the singer was right, and wrote
an article on Anglo-American rivalries which appeared in *Left*,
The Crisis and *Politics*. The colonial issue, as things were going,
he wrote to Dobson, with American senators calling for United
States control of the West Indies, might mean that the British
would 'fight their next war with the USA'.[3] Certainly, the Americans had become interested in Africa. The University of Pennsylvania produced for the Office of Strategic Services a series of
handbooks, under the guidance of the noted Austrian anthro-
pologist Hans Wieschhoff, and various groups tried to stimulate

public interest in the continent. Certain of the business magazines, such as *Fortune*, looked at Africa and found it fair in 'the American century'. Officers of the Phelps-Stokes Fund created the Committee on Africa, the War, and Peace Aims which held hearings within a month of American entry into the war. Testimony was accepted from Africans, among them Francis Nkrumah and Ako Adjei, and the results were published in 1942 with the title *The Atlantic Charter and Africa from an American Standpoint*. The somewhat suspect Council on African Affairs, Inc., also organised a conference in April 1944, for which Nkrumah did much of the preparatory work. This Council resulted from a meeting between Robeson and Max Yergan in London shortly before the war. The singer was on his way from West Africa and, several years before, Yergan had ended a fifteen-year stint (1921–36) as secretary for the (Coloured) Young Men's Christian Association in South Africa. They established an International Committee on African Affairs at 8 West 40th Street in New York and collected a respectable board of directors, among them Ralph Bunche, Channing Tobias, Mordecai Johnson, Réné Maran and Leonard Barnes. In 1943, they were joined by Alphaeus Hunton, described by DuBois as the 'son of the greatest Negro secretary the American Y M C A ever had; himself a Doctor of Philosophy in English, and a professor for seventeen years at Howard University'. The wealthy supporter of leftwing causes, Frederick V. Field, supposedly footed the bills.*

---

* Yergan and Hunton have had interesting careers. Yergan had lectured on the Ethiopian question at the National Negro Congress in Chicago in February 1936 and was one of the sponsors of Padmore's I A S B. Today he is a principal figure in various anti-communist movements and an apparent supporter of the present South African regime, whose militant opposition to communist causes he approves. It was not always so: in 1936 he explained that 'capitalist trusts divide up the spoils and repartition the world among themselves'. (See the *Official Proceedings and Resolutions of the NNC*, Chicago, February 14–16, 1936, and Yergan's *Gold and Poverty in South Africa*, International Industrial Relations Institute, The Hague and New York, 1938; also *Negro Worker*, May–June 1936.) For Hunton, who went to Ghana and until his recent deportation filled the late Dr DuBois's position as editor of the projected *Encyclopedia Africana*, see his *Decision in Africa*, New York 1954. The council is described in both DuBois, *In Battle for Peace*, New York 1952, and Padmore, *Pan-Africanism or Communism?*. During the Korean War it was placed on the United States Attorney-General's subversive organisations list.

Americans were beginning to see Africans in appreciable numbers during the war. The small trickle of students had quickened, and not all of them were directed to the little colleges and seminaries of the Negro South. Their number was still small, but their influence was considerable. They were in touch with WASU through their own body, the African Students' Association of North America. The Nigerian contingent, led by K. O. Mbadiwe, purchased a Harlem property in 1942, and Africa House became headquarters for those visiting the city. To this place came such young men as Nkrumah, who, in 1943, while a graduate student and Fante language informant at the University of Pennsylvania, met C. L. R. James there. James (who was in the United States under his Johnson pseudonym) provided Nkrumah with a letter of introduction to Padmore.[4]

The Council on African Affairs meeting was held in New York on April 14, 1944. About a hundred attended, including at least five Africans and the representatives of the Liberian, Belgian, French and Soviet delegations in New York. Two proposals seemed promising: the establishment of an African press centre and an international African development authority. The first arose from a suggestion made by K. A. B. Jones-Quartey,* a class-mate of Nkrumah and the representative of the African Students' Association journal, *The African Interpreter*. The Africans present reacted initially with some suspicion when Max Yergan raised the matter of the development authority. What role would Africans play in it, Nkrumah enquired. But this was smoothed over. The fact was, even the communists at this time did not believe Africans could rule themselves *instanter*. Benjamin Davis, latest of the American Negroes to rise to high office in the Communist Party, had declared: 'Most of Africa is not ready for self-government, but nothing will teach these people faster than a war for world-wide democracy for which they provide the battleground.'[5]

In Britain, too, the victory at last seemed clear, and groups began to moot the postwar fate of Africa. Dr Harold Moody, after considerable discussion, decided to convene another conference on the colonial question, the first the LCP had sponsored in a

* Today a member of the University of Ghana faculty, the biographer of Azikiwe and the best known student of the West African press.

decade. The National Council for Civil Liberties Overseas Sub-Committee drafted the background paper (later published as *Civil Liberties and the Colonies*, April 1945). It was a sober statement of colour bar in employment and education, of unjust taxation and restriction of speech and movement. Wallace-Johnson's case was cited. The conferees called for an end to discrimination in Britain, for immediate steps towards colonial freedom, such as African majorities on West Coast legislative councils, and for progress reports to the (hopefully forthcoming) United Nations Organisation. A "Charter for Coloured Peoples" was sent to the Prime Minister, who replied that their concern was misplaced. Moody demurred, this time taking Padmore's position that the colossal Russian successes had come about largely because the Soviet Union had solved the race relations problem of the old czarist regime.[6]

Sometime late in 1944, Padmore and others formed the Pan-African Federation (PAF), the last and most ambitious of the 'pan' bodies he was connected with. Two British Guianans, a physician named Peter M. Milliard and T. R. Makonnen, both of Manchester, were the principal lights. The IASB, the Kikuyu Central Association, the Sierra Leone section of the African Youth League, the Association of Students of African Descent in Dublin (principally the work of Jaja Wachuku, later to become Nigerian Foreign Secretary), and a number of British Negro groups were affiliates. The LCP and WASU, significantly, were not. Milliard and Makonnen had extensive plans for adult education, consumer and producers' co-operatives, trust and banking facilities and an African authors' library.* Padmore had considerable doubt about

---

* Makonnen, according to Randy Dixon, a war correspondent for the *Courier*, intended building a large hotel in London's West End which would cater to coloured tourists after the war. Dixon wrote that 'Dr Thomas Makonnie [*sic*], enterprising restaurateur of Manchester', employed over forty persons at his popular establishment, a sort of northern Palm Court, which offered varied cuisine, banquet rooms and a miniature symphonic orchestra. Makonnen described himself as an Ethiopian graduate of Cornell and Manchester Universities who had worked for three years with the Texas YMCA. He was well known to coloured American troops, 'tan Yanks' as they were known in the Negro press (Pittsburg *Courier*, October 14, 1944).

the viability of such enterprises, but he went along, in effect ending his IASB by merging it with the new Manchester body.

Their first move was to bring out a series of booklets for the Pan-African Institute, the PAF's publications branch. The first three titles which came off Makonnen's press were Kenyatta's *Kenya— Land of Conflict*, a chapter from Nancy Cunard's *Negro Anthology* (Raymond Michelet's "African Empires and Civilizations"), and a manuscript by Eric Williams, *The Negro in the Caribbean*.[7] Williams's manuscript had no market, though Dobson had asked Padmore if he would like to take it in hand for possible publication in England. Dobson felt that, as it stood, with prices quoted in dollars and so on, it was more readily intelligible to Americans.[8] Williams was a rising young academic at Howard University by this time, already a consultant on Caribbean problems. Padmore decided to bring out the manuscript himself, and he prevailed upon the Pan-African Federation for the necessary £200.

Padmore also tried to publish a manuscript written by a Gold Coast physician, S. D. Cudjoe, after the author's first visit home in seventeen years. It was, Padmore told Dobson, 'the best book I have yet seen by an African. . . . I am glad to see the native African putting forward Africa's case so ably as this fellow has done. No longer will the Tories be able to say that the blacks are happy in their primitiveness.'[9] Dr Cudjoe finally published the booklet himself as *Aids to African Autonomy*. He thanked Padmore for having read the fuller original manuscript and quoted from *White Man's Duty*. It is an excellently written and telling anti-colonial tract and it is difficult to understand why it never achieved much notoriety. Padmore's estimate of it was eminently sound. He later tried to get Dobson to publish the manuscript of another African, his former enemy Clements Kadalie. When this remarkable Nyasaland trade unionist wrote his version of the ICU's history, he sent it to Padmore, who told Professor DuBois that no one in South Africa would touch it. Padmore had no luck in Britain either, nor was DuBois any more successful in America. Dobson remembers seeing the work, but has no idea what happened to it.[10]

In October 1944, Padmore wrote to Dobson, saying that he had been over to France, presumably as a correspondent, which never was his forte. He always preferred the assignment which took him to his library (his one vice was book-buying) where, among the Blue Books, reports of commissions and press clippings, he could write a background piece. On only one occasion did an article of his scoop the press, and its news value depended on another reporter's action. In March 1945, he sent a despatch to the *Defender*, which was printed in the issue of March 24, saying that the Duke of Windsor had resigned the governorship of the Bahamas because of the intransigence of the local planter aristocracy and the cowardice of the Colonial Office, which had failed to support his efforts to alleviate the conditions of black workers. He had been resisted at all turns, despite the recommendations made by the royal commission appointed to enquire into the riots of 1942. Padmore drew an analogy with the fate of Sir Murchison Fletcher, the governor of Trinidad whom he had written about in 1938. This report was picked up by the New York correspondent of the London *Daily Mirror*, who surely must have been one of the few whites then reading the Negro American press, and cabled home, where it made a considerable splash.[11] For a lifetime in journalism, though, this hardly constituted dash.

Early in 1945, as a result of the ILO deliberations in Philadelphia,[12] a meeting was held in London to create a world trade union assembly. The conference opened in County Hall on Tuesday, February 5, and immediately became bogged down in 'peripheral' issues, such as colonialism. The British government, rather unwisely but of necessity, had allowed seven colonial trade unionists to attend—among them Wallace-Johnson, who remarked that he had been flown to London because the British knew the game was up, 'the years of their oppression are numbered'.[13] These men wished to discuss the peace settlement and the fate of colonial workers, while the great power representatives hoped to avoid such divisive matters. The proceedings of the conference indicate that the coloured colonials gave a good account of themselves. Wallace-Johnson, Ken Hill of Jamaica, J. A. Garba-Jahumpa of Gambia, Hubert Crichlow of British Guiana, Joe Annan of the Gold Coast, Timothy Bankole of Nigeria: all were articulate, aggressive and unimpressed. Time and again they recurred to a few basic points: colour bar, forced labour, pass laws, wage differentials. All these had to come to an end. They urged British labour to accept its responsibilities in the colonies and quoted Marx's dictum that 'labour in the white skin cannot free itself while labour in the black skin is enslaved'. Colonialism was just as objectionable as fascism. The conference message to the 'Big Three' who were meeting at Yalta talked of a liberated Europe. What of those unfree elsewhere? The creation of legitimate trade unions and the institution of wages boards in the colonies could not be delayed. Bankole moved that Paragraph 25 of a 33-point Declaration be amended to force the colonial powers to set a time for the attainment of colonial freedom, rather than merely talk of 'all possible speed'. This motion, after considerable debate, was defeated. Finally, Joe Annan pleaded for a West African federation within any world federation of unions.[14]

At the conclusion of the conference on Saturday, February 17, Ken Hill and Wallace-Johnson were asked to stay on to assist in drafting a colonial programme for the British TUC. This meeting at Transport House on February 26 signalled organised British labour's new involvement with colonial workers.[15] At the end of the month, they were invited up to Manchester, where they conferred with the IASB and others in the Pan-African Federation. There, Padmore suggested it was time for another Pan-African Conference—the first since 1927—which, with sufficient publicity, might convene in Paris that September. Through an American Red Cross worker, a Negro named Gordon Gray, they hoped to get American support for such a meeting.[16] So far as I know, this was the first proposal for the Fifth Congress. Padmore had talked about one in the mid-1930s. DuBois had hoped for yet another after his fourth convention in 1927, but nothing had happened. Depression, war and the struggle for survival had preoccupied black Americans, and their colonial brethren could do nothing without assistance.

Two weeks later, Padmore noted that the provisional committee had drafted a manifesto and sent a copy to the NAACP. Invitations were mailed to fraternal bodies around the world. In line with the Atlantic Charter and the Yalta deliberations, the delegates intended urging a United Nations developmental body for Africa, steps towards African independence, and the elimination of illiteracy and commodity price instability.[17] From this time Padmore's concentration on African affairs became noticeable. According to Subasinghe:

His association with colonial students living in London, particularly those from Africa and the West Indies, expanded very rapidly during the latter part of the war. Many students and others came to him for help and advice. Jomo Kenyatta was a very close friend of his during this period. So was Nkrumah, who arrived in London from the United States during the war. Nkrumah came very much under George's influence during the latter part of the war and I think this influence continued up to the very end of his life. During this period I also began to detect a change in George's political emphasis. He was becoming more and more cynical about the role of the working class and the so-called anti-imperialists of imperialist countries. He began to advocate the theory that the liberation of the colonial peoples was their own responsibility and that they had to rely on their own resources for their emancipation. Following from this he became more and more interested in the Pan-African movement although he was critical of some of the early Pan-Africans. He held Professor DuBois of the United States in great respect and veneration.[*18]

The next step taken by the PAF was to present a manifesto to the great powers, whose representatives were in San Francisco organising the United Nations. This averred that the 'Big Three' had shown faith in the Atlantic Charter and now must apply it to Africa. Both the economic and the political needs of Africa demanded recognition; mass education was imperative. All these rights had been earned by Africans during war service. The manifesto was signed by Makonnen for the IASB; J. E. Taylor and E. J. Du Plan for the Negro Welfare Centers; Peter Milliard for the Negro Association; T. Dowuona-Hyde for the Anglo-Negro Fellowship;

* Proof of this veneration may be seen in the telegram which Peter Abrahams and he sent to Dr and Mrs DuBois on their fiftieth wedding anniversary, May 10, 1946: 'We rejoice with you. Allah be praised. He has rewarded your labours on behalf of your people with greatest gifts, a loving devoted wife, daughter, grand-daughter, and has preserved your life to see your beloved intellectual child Pan-Africanism grow and flourish far and wide. Long labours are fully rewarded. May you live to see final victory. On this happy, auspicious occasion we, your colonial admiring disciples, salute you and wish God's blessing on your household.' (Copy sent to author from DuBois archives by Dr Herbert Aptheker.)

Kenyatta for the KCA; A. A. Mossell, J. Nurse, A. Hassan and B. Roderick for the United Committee of Colonial and Colonial [*sic*, probably Colonial and Coloured] Peoples; Dr Moody for the LCP; and K. A. Chunchie, C. B. Clarke, Desmond Buckle, Sampson Morris, Wallace-Johnson, Peter Blackman and R. W. Beoku-Betts.[19] Curiously, Padmore's name did not appear, though the first draft which was printed in the April edition of the LCP *News-letter* carried his signature. Though he was instrumental in drafting this document, Padmore was pessimistic about its effect. In the *Defender* that month, he wrote that Europe was without capital to spare, and anxious not to let the Yankees in the door during their period of embarrassment. Until colonial peoples had direct access to the United Nations, he doubted there would be any fundamental changes.* Nor should anyone imagine that the outcome of the British general election would benefit the peoples of the British empire. The fact of a massive swing to the Parliamentary Labour Party by the electorate meant nothing, he wrote in the October *Crisis*, for that political party was influenced more by Kipling than by Marx.

The Labour Party victory nevertheless was attended by an Open Letter from the PAF. Prime Minister Attlee was informed that 'to condemn the Imperialism of Germany, Japan and Italy while condoning that of Britain would be more than dishonest. It would be a betrayal of the sacrifice and sufferings and the toil and sweat of the common people of Britain. All Imperialism is evil.'[20] Attlee was reminded that 'the victory of the common man here is the victory of the common man in Africa, Asia and other colonial lands. ... It is the challenge of our time that you, Mr Attlee, and your Government should give the Socialist answer to the Tory imperialism of Mr Churchill's "What we have we hold".' 'What will your answer be?' the PAF demanded.[21] Padmore did not discount those members of the British public who over the years had supported his causes, but he saw them as individuals powerless to change the conservatism of the British public.[22] He had concluded by 1945 that colonial problems could be settled only by colonial peoples. Yet, somewhat

---

* This was a strong point with Padmore, one he came to feel more and more as the postwar decade rolled on, until finally he complained that Nkrumah, by then identified as the African saviour, was not seizing power fast enough.

inconsistently, the PAF momentarily considered putting forward its own parliamentary candidates, among them Kenyatta (described in the LCP *Newsletter* of July 1945 as 'a Kenya chieftain and lecturer in Anthropology'), Milliard, Moody and Padmore. That Padmore would consider standing for membership in the imperial legislature, after a decade of refusals to the ILP selectors, seems a curious lapse of judgement.

These documents drafted, a call went out for an All-Colonial Peoples' Conference to meet in London on June 10. This was the work of the PAF, the Federation of Indian Associations in Britain, WASU, the Ceylon Students' Association and the Burma Association.[23] The conferees called for the liquidation of imperialism, the application of the Atlantic Charter to the colonies, the release of colonial political prisoners, the formation of a World Colonial Council, with representatives from the colonies, to formulate policy, supervise elections and generally oversee the devolution of imperial control, a universal end to the colour bar and guarantees that Italian and Japanese controlled territories would not revert to colonial status.

The draft memorandum of the charter contains certain interesting observations. The authors were certain that 'for them the destruction of Nazism signifies not an end but a beginning . . . for those who had tolerated and even connived at imperialism with its colour bars, segregation and denial of the most elementary human rights . . . are beginning to learn by experience that these evils know no frontiers. They have seen how Nazi Germany, taking its inspiration from the technique of domination perfected by other imperialist powers of the West, tried to force upon the nations of Europe the same chains of bondage which imperialism so far had reserved for the colonial masses.' They observed that the various declarations in San Francisco offered 'no hint on the future status of colonial countries'; indeed they were 'in complete contradiction to what is happening in subject countries like India, British, French and Belgian colonies, where thousands of patriots are languishing behind prison bars . . . where shootings and floggings on the Nazi pattern are the order of the day. The Colonial peoples may, therefore, be forgiven if they discount the exalted phraseology of allied statesmen.' It closed with the confident assertion that great consequences would flow from the devolution of empires. 'On the one hand, by creating conditions favourable to the free development of subject nations, it will give an impetus to world trade and prosperity. On the other, by removing all inter-imperialist rivalries which are the root cause of wars, it will provide solid foundations for the building of free and equal nations, thus ensuring world peace which all humanity so ardently desires.'[24]

Jaundiced observers of postwar events will find this an incredibly naïve document, which would be unfair, for all sorts of persons reflected these views in 1945. Freedom would mean development and development would mean world peace. This oversimplified version of Lenin's oversimple thesis must not be blamed on those who drafted this timely memorandum. Upon adopting this statement, some delegates called for another conference, an All-Negro one, to be held in September in association with the NAACP. Out of this second meeting, Padmore wrote, might come plans for a Pan-African convention *in Africa* before very long.[25]

During the same month Nigerian civil servants and technical workers struck to protest against the cost of living and the side-tracking of African aspirations at the end of the war. Chief A. Soyemi Coker of the Trades Union Congress–Nigeria thanked the PAF for its immediate aid.[26] Padmore was the principal speaker at a WASU meeting in Conway Hall in July, called to denounce the suppression of Azikiwe's newspapers. He delivered platitudes—'It is occasions like these that test men's souls'—but they were applauded. Later that year, he was invited to address the WASU study group.[27]

It was at this point, according to his Indian friend, Kumria, and the Ceylonese Ambassador, Subasinghe, that Padmore began to neglect Asian concerns in favour of African affairs. Though from time to time he wrote about events in South East Asia after the end of the war, increasingly he seemed aloof from, even impatient with, non-African considerations. Indian independence was to have several consequences for those concerned to free Africa. While on the one hand Indians could devote attention to the cause of independence elsewhere in the colonial world, on the other hand they often were too concerned with their own problems to think very much about colonialism in Africa. Kumria found that, despite his efforts, a gap steadily widened between Indians and Africans in London after 1947. However, early in 1948, Padmore, Douglas Rogers of the British Centre for Colonial Freedom and Kundan Lal Jalie of Swaraj House announced that Swaraj House henceforth would be a general anti-colonial meeting place open to all groups.[28] Indians were not the only ones put aside by the West African enthusiasts. The then secretary of the Congress of Peoples Against Colonialism, Mrs Mary Klopper, recalls that Padmore was very much on the sidelines of that organisation and almost totally immersed in Gold Coast affairs, despite his long friendship with Brockway's group.[29]

The LCP *Newsletter* of September reported that 'a meeting was held at the Pan-African Institute, 66 Oxford Road, Manchester, on Sunday, 12th August, to discuss preliminaries regarding a Congress to be held in this country during the month of October next—and not September, as was formerly stated. Representatives were present from the various coloured organizations in England and the Chairman was Dr Milliard of Trinidad.' Padmore, Abrahams, Kenyatta and Makonnen joined Milliard's provisional committee, which did a great deal of work, contacting as many as possible of the Negro organisations on three continents, creating an agenda, arranging for housing and accreditation and insuring publicity.

One other activist joined the group, soon becoming, with Padmore, co-political secretary. This was Francis K. Nkrumah, who arrived in London in May with a letter of introduction to Padmore from C. L. R. James. Padmore and Nkrumah were instantly attracted to each other: they felt like brothers. A fourteen-year collaboration had begun. Interestingly enough, Nkrumah did not make such an impression on many who knew Padmore well, several in fact saying that, though they must have met Nkrumah, they had no recollection of him; indeed, one remarked that her only memory was of a shy, smiling young man who stood on the sidelines at social gatherings and occasionally joked with girls.

Padmore saw much more. Very early on, he seems to have transferred his hopes for a united free Africa from Azikiwe to Nkrumah, though at times he grew impatient even with the latter. This is not an argument for the 'man behind the scenes' thesis which is so popular in Padmore's case. He was older, but only by three years; he was immensely more experienced and cosmopolitan, but, unlike the younger man, Padmore was too sophisticated, too prone to doubt, too humorous to match Nkrumah's single-mindedness. Though Padmore wrote in 1928 that he was dedicating his life so that children might see a better world, this was a student's private jotting, the only such self-conscious statement that I have found. Nkrumah's writings, on the other hand, are full of such statements, and they are not to be understood figuratively, even if his practice did not rise to his ideal. Professor John Phillips, the first of Nkrumah's European supporters to leave Accra in sorrow, put it fairly when he wrote: 'While not wishing to belittle George Padmore's contribution, I believe that he was credited by some and blamed by others for rather more than that for which he was responsible. He cannot be considered as alternately Nkrumah's essential inspiration for all that was wise or all that was held to be the reverse. He had an influence and was a source of help to Nkrumah, but it was not his but Nkrumah's genius that inspired and waged the fight for the political, economic and spiritual freedom of Africa.'[30]

Nkrumah, by any standard, was no commonplace anti-colonialist; he was a revolutionary. Padmore introduced him to most people on the left, put him in touch with wasu, may even have sent him to members of the British Communist Party, though this seems unlikely. One of Nkrumah's former Lincoln University classmates, Ako Adjei (whose death penalty he later commuted to a lengthy term of imprisonment), was already studying law in London when Nkrumah arrived. They met by accident on a bus, the first of many encounters which soon gave Nkrumah a solid base for his next move, the creation of a secretariat for West African affairs, a notion much approved by Padmore. Within a month, then, Nkrumah was a joint secretary of the Congress organising committee, working at all hours to prepare the agenda and invite delegates. 'We used to sit in his small kitchen', Nkrumah later wrote of Padmore, 'the wooden table completely covered by papers, a pot of tea which we always forgot until it had been made two or three hours, and George typing at his small typewriter so fast that the papers were churned out as though they were being rolled off a printing press.'[31] This table, according to Padmore's nephew, later was sent to Ghana at Nkrumah's request.[32]

The actual announcement of the conference came from Sampson Morris of the lcp who wrote in the *Defender* of September 8 that it would convene in London. Professor DuBois also had been trying to organise another Pan-African congress. Two questions, however, had vexed him. How could delegates secure transport? And, in any case, should overseas Negroes plan yet another African meeting?[33] So when he learned of these British developments, he wished the conferees (who were to convene in London on October 15) well. WASU also had doubts about the advisability of yet another Pan-African conference on foreign soil. In a letter to DuBois they said:

> The idea of a conference of African nations and all people of African descent throughout the world is both useful and timely. Perhaps it is even long overdue. But we observe that four of such Pan-African conferences had been held in the past, all within recent memory, and that the one at present under discussion will be the fifth. It is unfortunate that all these important conferences should have been held not only outside Africa, but in European capitals. This point is significant and should deserve our careful attention. . . . Our Executive Committee are certainly not in favour of this or any future Pan-African conference being held anywhere in Europe. We do rather suggest the Republic of Liberia as perhaps an ideal choice. . . . We have good reason to believe that the Government of Liberia would welcome this idea, and would give us the encouragement and diplomatic assistance that might be necessary to ensure success.[34]

On September 29, DuBois announced that the NAACP was sending him to London. He obviously was pleased, though at his age expected nothing too spectacular: 'There is no reason to think that the present Congress is going to be more "Pan-African" than the others.' Previously, only educated Africans attended such gatherings, but now a delegation of African trade unionists was in the United Kingdom. Padmore was in charge of planning but, because he was unable to get much publicity, the congress would have to be considered a preliminary one, DuBois thought.* Certainly, the

---

* In this article, DuBois called Padmore the nephew of Henry Sylvester Williams, the Trinidad barrister responsible for convening the first Pan-African conference in August 1900, a meeting which DuBois had attended to deliver the famous dictum: 'The problem of the twentieth century is the color line' (see Legum, *Pan-Africanism*). To my knowledge Padmore was not related to the lawyer, though it would have been satisfying to detect a kinship. Perhaps the elderly DuBois saw himself as the link between these men and their conferences, a pardonable fancy.

NAACP wanted a 'real' congress in the near future.[35] The convening committee, especially Padmore, agreed with DuBois that the
conference 'should be merely a preliminary one to a greater, more
representative Congress to be held some time next year . . .'. But,
they added, it seemed a good idea to meet now, since so many
colonials were in Paris for the World Trade Union Conference
which created the World Federation of Trade Unions (WFTU)
and might be expected to come to Manchester easily. One of the
colonials who had gone to Paris was Wallace-Johnson, who again
contrived to raise the colonial issue. His call for unity across the
colour line was embodied in the WFTU charter, but he was unable
to get a colonial department established, though the executive did
assure him that it would give immediate attention to the issues he
raised. His condemnation of the South African government for its
refusal to let non-whites have passports to attend the conference
was moved by Curran, the representative of the American Congress
of Industrial Organisations (CIO), seconded by Papworth, representing the British Trades Union Congress (TUC), and carried
unanimously. Wallace-Johnson had at least these verbal victories
to his credit when he crossed the Channel again that autumn.[36]

The Pan-African conference finally opened on Monday, October
15, in the Chorlton Town Hall, Manchester, with about a hundred
delegates present.* The Lord Mayor of Manchester, Alderman
W. P. Jackson, who was introduced by Dr Milliard with suitable
reminders of the role played by Manchester cotton-mill workers
during the American Civil War, greeted the delegates. If this did
not put an official gloss on the proceedings, it certainly helped to
legitimise things. In the hall, which was decorated with the flags of
Liberia, Haiti and Ethiopia, Marcus Garvey's widow, Mrs Amy
Ashwood Garvey, chaired the first session on the colour problem in
Britain. Their grievances were familiar to anyone who studied the
LCP *Newsletter*: job opportunities ashore and at sea, the support of
illegitimate children fathered by Negro Americans, and discrimin-
atory treatment by the police. Nigerian WASU delegate, F. O. B.
Blaize, summed up: 'If the British people think they have the right
to live in Africa, then we have the right to stay here. We have the
right to get together and see that something is done for us here.'

* Abrahams later exuberantly claimed double this figure (*New Leader*,
October 20, 1945).

De Graft Johnson, representing the Coloured Peoples' Association, Edinburgh, admitted that the African 'student class in Great Britain had cut itself aloof from the general body of coloured people in Great Britain, and that this had made the struggle more difficult'. As a student he had from time to time taken an active interest in the colour problem, but pointed out that students sometimes were treated with an air of suspicion.

On the Tuesday, the session devoted to imperialism in North and West Africa was chaired by DuBois. Nkrumah was the rapporteur and Padmore introduced the chairman, stressing the vigour and liveliness which DuBois displayed, his mind 'younger and more alive than many a youth's'. Early on, the new note was sounded by Joe Annan, one of the Gold Coast trade unionists who had attended the February assembly of world trade unionists. 'I am here as a workman, a man who wields tools, a man who knows no colour. I want you to feel that nothing we can do here is of any avail unless we are in a position to implement the resolutions that we are going to make. . . . So I suggest that before this Congress breaks up on Sunday we set up administrative machinery to cope with the difficulties which lie ahead of us. My workers have given me this mandate: to inform you that they are prepared to spend their last penny in order to maintain an office in London. That is a practical issue.' Nkrumah had this in mind when he later wrote that at this conference 'we shot into the limbo the gradualist aspirations of our African middle classes and intellectuals and expressed the solid down-to-earth will of our workers, trade unionists, farmers and peasants who were decisively represented at Manchester, for independence'. Even so, education and educated persons kept intruding into the discussion. In Padmorean fashion, Chief Soyemi Coker declaimed: 'It is by scholarship that Russia rose to be the Great Power to be reckoned with that she is today.' The session ended with a wry statement by the Nigerian journalist, Magnus Williams, the representative of Azikiwe's NCNC: 'The Colonial Office has always told us, by words and implication, that there is a happy land: and we have always answered "far, far away". We have come to this Congress to decide and enforce the means by which we shall make that happy land our own.'

On October 17, the decision to appoint chairmen for each session was rescinded and Padmore declared DuBois permanent chairman, 'as a token of esteem and respect'. At this session it became apparent that most Africans did not know much about Africa. Garba-Jahumpa said: 'We are here to learn about all our peoples from all over the world. . . . The Congress must resolve to set up somewhere in the world a central council which would keep in touch with the whole of the African world and know what is going on.' Their discussion of Ethiopian affairs demonstrated this woeful ignorance, for delegates seemed to believe that Somalis desired annexation by Ethiopia, a territorial ambition some urged the Congress to support. Only some unnamed 'extreme socialists' at the conference seemed to know anything about actual conditions in the horn of Africa. The Trinidadian oil worker, John Rojas (now a senator of Trinidad and Tobago), saw the conference as 'a master link in bringing together Afro-West Indians and Africans and other peoples of African descent, thus affording more clearly an opportunity to understand the problems of each other, which after all are fundamentally the same'. Another trade unionist, D. M. Harper of British Guiana, said that conditions were bad at home but nothing like what he now learned of Africa. 'I must confess I have done a little reading but I have never imagined that the conditions in those countries were as bad as I have heard here.'

Altogether, the Congress passed resolutions on West Africa, the Congo and North Africa, East Africa, the Union of South Africa, the three British Protectorates, the West Indies (and a supplemental one, urging West Indian federation, offered by the late Marcus Garvey's UNIA), another on the three black independent states, one pertaining to Ethiopia alone, one on the plight of coloured seamen in England, one on race relations in the United Kingdom and a lengthy final one concerning South West Africa.

Delegates had instructed their officers to implement all resolutions passed by the Congress, which were summed up in Nkrumah's "Declaration to the Colonial Workers, Farmers and Intellectuals". He rather ungraciously argued that the conference was important because 'for the first time the delegates who attended it were practical men and men of action and not, as was the case at the four previous conferences, merely idealists contenting themselves with writing theses but quite unable or unwilling to take any active part in dealing with the African problem. Like Garveyism, the first four conferences were not born of indigenous African consciousness.'[37] Nkrumah stressed that the seizure of political power was 'the first step towards, and the necessary prerequisite to, complete social, economic and political emancipation'. The strike and the boycott were the available weapons, but, unless colonial intellectuals awoke to their own responsibilities, the masses would not realise their strength. 'Today there is only one road to effective action— the organisation of the masses. And in that organisation the educated Colonials must join. Colonial and Subject Peoples of the World—Unite!'[38]

The final session 'was given over to a crowded mass meeting, marked by the exchange of many fraternal greetings'. DuBois was elected International President, and given a silver cigarette box and a pledge of solidarity with the NAACP. Moreover, one of DuBois's views took effect—during its centenary in 1947, Liberia was to be host for a sixth congress.[39] Padmore proposed that greetings also be sent to 'the masses of India', and a like statement was devoted to the peoples of Indonesia and Vietnam. Cables were received from the Gold Coast Aborigines' Rights Protection Society, from Professor D. D. T. Jabavu and the secretary of the African National Congress in South Africa, from the editor of the *Daily Gleaner*, Kingston, Jamaica, from the Indian Associations of Great Britain, from segments of the British Communist Party, the Socialist Vanguard Group, the Common Wealth Party and the ILP. (McNair attended as a fraternal delegate.)

On his final day in England, DuBois went down to London, where he stayed with Dr Clarke. A dinner party, comprising DuBois, Clarke, G. Ashie Nikoi, a delegate who was in the United Kingdom as a representative of the Gold Coast cocoa farmers, and Padmore, went to a Chinese restaurant in Soho, where Padmore acted as toastmaster. They then put DuBois on his plane for the United States.[40] The American dean of Pan-Africanism returned to the United States convinced that something new and important had occurred. He was aware of his own aloofness and the handicap it placed upon him. 'My leadership was a leadership solely of ideas. I never was, nor ever will be, personally popular', he had written in *Dusk of Dawn*.[41] But, in London, he had seen young Africans who had this flair. There was a new colonial abroad, he wrote in the *Defender*. Unlike those at the 1921 congress, who wasted time giving advice to Negro Americans, these Africans were too busy to concern themselves with extra-continental affairs. There was no more pride in being 'French' or 'Belgian', no more interest in contrasting their style with that of the crude Americans. They were, perhaps, a trifle melodramatic, but then most of them were workers, not middle-class sophisticates. The conference had been overweighted on the West African side, DuBois thought: South Africa was 'too inadequately represented to make it certain just what her demands are', and, though natives of Uganda and Kenya were present, both men had been away from home too long to be representative. West Africa, however, had presented a real bloc.[42]

Almost without exception, the white press ignored this conference. The *New Leader*, because McNair had attended, was the exception. This socialist weekly and the Negro American press remain the historian's best sources for the proceedings. Unfortunately, their contemporary readers were powerless to convey the sense of the convention to the wider public in Britain and America. One of the significant events in the postwar world went unremarked to its conclusion.

7

Gold Coast Ascendant

NKRUMAH was appointed secretary of the working committee which the Fifth Congress had authorised. Though PAF remained in Manchester, the committee was located in Padmore's London apartment. However, Nkrumah was not content to stop at this. Soon after the conference, he says he was approached by other West Africans, such as Wallace-Johnson, who suggested the establishment of a West African secretariat. This fell in with his own desires and he accepted the secretaryship of this new body, the West African National Secretariat (WANS).*

The LCP *Newsletter* of April 1946 noted that 'the first volume of a West African paper made its appearance last week in London, where it is printed and published. It is a monthly paper and is the organ of "The West African National Secretariat", whose offices are at 94 Gray's Inn Road. The Chairman of this body is Mr I. T. A. Wallace-Johnson, and the secretary Mr F. N. Kwame Nkrumah. We sincerely wish the new venture every success.' But the *New African* soon failed.[1] However, Nkrumah was able to convene another conference at the end of August 1946. Representatives of French Africa also attended this meeting, which was called jointly by WASU and WANS. There delegates reaffirmed the goals of the

* Another who prevailed upon Nkrumah was Bankole Awooner-Renner, a former Accra municipal councillor and editor of the *Gold Coast Leader*, who published an interesting pamphlet, *West African Soviet Union*, calling for the unity of all West Africans and a constitutional approach to the nationalities question similar to that of the Soviet Union. Much of his material was reprinted from wartime issues of the *New Statesman* and *Defender*, but it was timely, very much in the fashion of Padmore's own *How Russia Transformed Her Colonial Empire*.

Manchester Congress, and acknowledged that a West African federation was an indispensable first step towards a Pan-Africa. There was no colour bar, as in East and Southern Africa, there was almost no land alienation, few European settlers, large populations and a vast area. In their opinion, the newly created West African trade unions would be the best base for WANS in Africa.[2] The conferees urged another meeting somewhere in West Africa the following year. Their ultimate aim, according to Padmore, was a United Socialist States of Africa,* which sounded remarkably like Awooner-Renner's goal.[3]

The conference never took place, as Nkrumah by that time had received a call to return home to work for the United Gold Coast Convention.[4] Years later, he recalled that his notion of African unity then meant West African unity.[5] In the end, WANS came to very little, despite Nkrumah's activity. 'In 1947 I received a circular letter appealing for funds from the West African National Secretariat, with headquarters in London, and run by a West Coaster educated in USA', wrote W. R. Crocker. 'Jobs are provided by organizations like this. . . . It is not necessary to assume, of course, that the job-holders are scoundrels. We can take it that the majority of them are sincere men. These particular organizations appear to have Communist associations. On the other hand, scoundrels can and do tack themselves on to such organizations. The main qualifications, after all, are a ready tongue and a persistence in vilifying government.'[6] The only British assistance which Nkrumah noted in this period came from various dedicated young ladies who volunteered their secretarial services. What had started out to bridge the gap between students and others became instead a welfare organisation concerned with West African seamen in British ports.

In the summer of 1946 the Free India Press asked Padmore to cover the Paris peace conference. Dorothy wrote to Daniel Guerin, George's socialist contact from pre-war days, to see whether he could put them up. 'If things were quite normal, we should not of course ask, but we ourselves are always putting people up because of the shortage of accommodation, and we understand that Paris is no easier than London', she wrote, somewhat defensively.[7] They

---

* Nkrumah, of course, in later years, after his access to power, decried regional arrangements as an obstacle to Pan-Africa.

crossed the Channel on July 28 and stayed throughout the deliberations of the great powers. Padmore passed around advance copies
of *How Russia Transformed Her Colonial Empire*, with the hope
that some continental sales might result. He wrote to Dobson that
the book had attracted great interest and that this market should
be explored.[8]

He did not see Guerin, for Dorothy's letter reached the Frenchman only on October 6, nor was he very fortunate in some of his
other searches for former friends. But, from a journalist's standpoint, Paris was lovely. One of his articles still remains a good
introduction to Vietnamese affairs, for Ho Chi Minh gave him an
interview in the private hotel where the French government had
placed him. Padmore's nephew, Dr Luke, suggested that the two
had known each other from Comintern days; this may be true,
though Padmore's references to Ho rather contradict the notion.
In any case, Ho, who had been in Paris since June for confidential
negotiations with the French government, spent two hours with
Padmore. One result was that Padmore became the unofficial
guardian of Viet-Minh interests in London, to which city Ho
despatched a representative for English language training.[9] The
article which Padmore wrote for the Chicago *Defender* is a model of
Padmoreana, a concise introduction to the Vietnam tangle, one
which holds up surprisingly well after nearly two decades of per-
sistent journalistic rediscovery of the situation in South East Asia.[10]
It demonstrated once again Nancy Cunard's contention that the
careful reader of the Negro press could be remarkably well-
informed about the affairs of the coloured, colonial world; she
added, however, that there was some doubt that this readership
existed.[11]

Part of the article was reprinted in the December issue of *Politics*
as "The Story of Viet Nam". Padmore played down Ho's communist associations, which brought him considerable censure from
MacDonald's readers.[12] Victor Serge accused Padmore of glossing
over Ho's affiliation and he demanded to know if Padmore really
believed Russia was a collection of free nationalities. Saul
Mendelson rebuked Padmore for being too important to say that
the French socialists sympathised with Ho. Padmore replied that
Vietnam was far from Moscow; Ho's revolt would not extend to
totalitarianism. And he decried the preoccupation with anti-

communism which seemed so tiresomely characteristic of the American leftwing socialists. In a letter to Guerin, Padmore wrote that 'my feeling about Ho Chi Minh's signing of the Modus Vivendi is that he hoped to gain a little time to arrange his forces, and that he was looking forward to the return of a Left Government at the coming elections in France. My opinion is that there is a wide opposition to any compromise with France among the Vietnamese people, and that they are quite prepared to take up the struggle once more for complete independence.'[13]

As for the peace conference, Padmore was dubious. True, it was more democratic than the 1919 deliberations in that city, he wrote. But, the new British Labour government displayed a tendency to fawn on the Americans in order to preserve the empire. The suggestion that Russia might intrude in African affairs—a reference to the idea that former Italian Libya be entrusted to the Soviet Union—had so frightened the British and American foreign ministers that the entire colonial issue was taken off the agenda. The cold war was shaping up, and Padmore disliked it.[14] He saw the trusteeship system as 'nothing more than a continuation of the mandates system inaugurated under the now defunct League of Nations, modified and refurnished to accommodate the conflicting ideologies of the Great Powers'.[15] It was, he wrote in the first issue of *Pan-Africa*, 'absurd to think that an imperialist war can finish in a non-imperialist peace'. And, he concluded, 'at Paris there is neither idealism nor morality'.[16] He watched the unfolding United Nations Organisation closely during the first year of peace, his scepticism growing daily as he read of a British Labour government aiding the French and the Dutch to recover their Asiatic possessions, while the Russo-American conflict grew day by day. In all this he saw little room for serious consideration of African affairs, except as an aspect of global strategy, and he again fretted that American preoccupation with strategic materiel would retard the African freedom movement.

In February 1946, a postwar counterpart of the old LAI appeared, calling itself the British Centre Against Imperialism. Fenner Brockway announced that similar centres would open in the Netherlands, France and America, to act as information points, links to legislators and guides to worker agitators. At their first meeting, Padmore spoke on "Africa and the West Indies", and referred to the Manchester Congress as a starting round in the fight. Many were most moved by a woman who said she had chosen celibacy rather than bring a black child into the present world.[17] The previous month Padmore had begun an interesting newsletter which lasted two years, quite a while as political ephemera go. *The Colonial Parliamentary Bulletin: A Monthly Record of the Colonies in Westminster* was produced at his flat in Cranleigh Street by the African Press Agency for the IASB. It carried advertisements— not of a leftwing nature, either—and was gleaned from *Hansard*.[18]

In the same period he assured his *Defender* readers that the second Labour government would combat racial discrimination in public places of accommodation, yet another illustration of his unwillingness to equate socialists and other whites. Like many people in England, Padmore tended to blame the presence of American troops for racial conflict. No doubt Americans ex- acerbated conditions, but they helped a large number of British people to formulate what they had vaguely suspected: that they dis- liked having to do with coloured people. According to Padmore, the government was going to act, largely at the urging of the PAF.[19] For the same cause, the PAF sponsored a rally at Old King's Hall in the Commercial Road towards the end of May to dramatise the need for democratic rights at home and abroad. Padmore chaired the meeting, announcing it was a start towards the end of the colour bar.[20]

While he was becoming more and more concerned with West African affairs after the war, to the exclusion of an active interest in events transpiring elsewhere on the continent, this did not happen overnight. Both Ethiopia, whose future relations with Britain seemed doubtful, and the Sudan, which was striving for freedom from the Anglo-Egyptian condominium, continued to exercise him. (In fact, his nephew has suggested that Padmore would have gone to the Sudan, had not events moved faster in the Gold Coast.) In the *Defender*, Padmore decried a world in which the victorious allies gave aid to Italy, but not to Italy's principal victim, Ethiopia, and he wrote up an interview with the representatives of Umma, the freedom party of the Arabic Sudan, when they came to London for talks with the government. He was on familiar terms with one delegate, Yacoub Osman, the thirty-five year old editor of *El Nile* (in 1964, Sudanese Ambassador to the Soviet Union), who had been one of his student friends in pre-war London.[21] On December 2, the LCP and PAF jointly sponsored an anti-colonial meeting at Holborn Hall. The speakers were Osman and Norman Stanley, the West Indian barrister who was in town to defend a Jamaican accused of murder. Fenner Brockway and Peter Abrahams also spoke.[22] As a member of the Coloured Writers' Association, Padmore had met the American novelist Richard Wright early in 1944. This acquaintance grew into a lasting friendship, and much information could, no doubt, be gleaned from their correspondence in the 1950s.*

Some money continued to come in from the sale of *How Russia Transformed Her Colonial Empire*. 'Thanks for the cheque and statement', he wrote to Dobson in March 1947. 'I must say that I was greatly surprised, for my relationships with publishers have not given me a very high regard for their integrity. On the other hand', he added, 'I am such a bad sort of business man, it might be all my own fault for being robbed by them.'[23] He was not, despite this disclaimer, all that inept in business matters. Indeed, Dobson thought Padmore was very forward where sale of his books was involved. This book was seized by the Gold Coast authorities in the early summer, a rather silly move, as it was available in Nigeria and the Colonial Secretary had agreed there was nothing against Africans reading widely. Dobson's firm appealed to the National Council for Civil Liberties,[24] and a question was raised in the House of Commons. 'Mr Skinnard asked the Secretary of State for the Colonies in what circumstances, and for what reasons, 200 copies of the book *How Russia Transformed Her Colonial Empire* were seized in the Gold Coast under the Customs Ordinance; whether he is aware that this book is in circulation in Nigeria; and whether he will take steps to allow it free circulation in the Gold Coast.' Creech Jones admitted that he was in the dark; another member, apparently even more puzzled, asked what the Russian empire was. Leslie

* Some other scholar may be allowed to examine the Wright papers in Paris. Because of my stated views on the irregularity of Dr Danquah's death in Ghana in 1965 (*New York Times*, February 21, 1965), Mrs Wright concluded I was unsympathetic to African aspirations and denied me access to the papers. For the public meeting which Wright addressed, see *Pan-Africa*, August 1947. This scarce periodical appeared in January of that year, edited by Makonnen, with Padmore a frequent contributor. Copies of his *How Russia Transformed . . .* were given to early subscribers.

Hale, Labour member for Oldham West, described the author as a 'distinguished British coloured subject of great authority and knowledge who, curiously enough, is by no means pro-Russian'. The consignment later was released. The episode probably demonstrates only the failure of the authorities of one colony to contact those of another, a commonplace event, especially in a system which expected the 'men on the spot' to take local initiative.[25]

In May, Padmore wrote about the spreading unrest in East Africa, and attacked the Colonial Secretary, Arthur Creech Jones, for the about-face which he had performed when he became Minister of State.[26] Attacks like this probably accounted for the coolness which Labourites such as Creech Jones and Rita Hinden felt towards Padmore.* However, Padmore had a new ally in the House of Commons, the above-mentioned Leslie Hale, who recalls:

> The only thing that I can remember clearly is that he was introduced to me by the late R. W. G. MacKay, who was then Member for Hull . . . he said George Padmore has got a lot of worries and you are interested in the colonies and can you deal with them, and I said all right, and I saw quite a lot of him for a time. I remember him saying, 'He is a very nice fellow but they say he has got a private line to Moscow', this being said half jestingly and half seriously and I said 'Do you mean it?' and he said, 'Well, no, but I wouldn't say it isn't possible.' Soon after that I took a flat in London which was off the Tottenham Court Road and my recollection is that George then was living in North London and at any rate he used to come along to see me at the flat usually at a fairly early hour in the morning and bring political problems. A lot of them were coming from Uganda. I had raised in the House of Commons some time before the question of some executions

---

* Padmore 'was able and very bright and certainly was of a very sharp intelligence. . . . I think his journalism was competent but often, I fancy, he designed his articles for the purposes he had in mind. He wrote a history regarding the West Coast of Africa but it is marred by what to me appear to be many distortions and prejudices. I never regarded him as an accurate historian. He was too concerned with proving the wickedness of imperialism which did not always exist.' (Letter, Creech Jones to author, 26th May, 1964.) 'We used to have many differences of opinion in writing because he was a near-communist or Trotskyist whereas I have always been a democratic socialist.' (Letter, Hinden to author, 14th May, 1964.)

for alleged ritual murder in what is now Ghana, which was a rather sensational Parliamentary event at the time and the executions were postponed and so-on and finally were a traditional British compromise of hanging two and not hanging the other two. . . . We worked together quite happily and the cases he brought to me were all genuine cases of genuine grievances being suffered by people in Africa.[27]

This relationship, according to Hale, lasted until Fenner Brockway came back into the House and 'became the very natural and very distinguished leader of the group interested in colonial affairs on the Labour back benches'.

On May 1, Dr Harold Moody was buried. Padmore was the PAF representative at the funeral, which marked the effective end of the LCP, which for sixteen years had tried so hard to seek reform within the British system.[28] Padmore had little to do with it after Moody's death, but Dorothy remained a member of the LCP editorial committee.

That same month, a delegation from the National Council of Nigeria and Cameroons (NCNC), headed by its president Azikiwe, arrived in London to protest against the imposition of the Richards Constitution in Nigeria. Padmore acted as press secretary and, in this post, put Zik's party into direct and lasting contact with Nkrumah's WANS, WASU (of which Nkrumah now was secretary), and PAF. Even though the NCNC had been represented at the Manchester Congress in 1945, it had not become involved in succeeding events. Now Zik endorsed the Congress's aims.[29] Padmore felt that the NCNC visit was useful.* The British press played it up, the public were aware that the Richards Constitution was detested in Nigeria, and the initiative seemed to be passing to the NCNC. Now, he wrote with characteristic bluntness, it was necessary for the party to create an honest leadership out of a welter of tribal and trade union bodies.[30]

---

* Professor Jones-Quartey, who wrote *A Life of Azikiwe*, unfortunately could not spend the additional time necessary to unravel the Padmore–Azikiwe relationship. (Letter, Jones-Quartey to author, November 12, 1965.) Dr Azikiwe declined to assist me in the same task. According to Jones-Quartey (page 186), the money raised to send this seven-man delegation was the subject of angry enquiry when they returned from their five-month stay in Britain.

Gold Coast Ascendant

But Nigeria was soon thrust aside by Gold Coast events. Nkrumah received the UGCC secretaryship offer (at Ako Adjei's urging), and, with Padmore's strenuous approval, accepted. As Brockway recalls, Padmore 'was a considerable influence in getting Nkrumah to go back to Ghana, despite the reactionary leadership of the Gold Coast nationalist movement'.[31] Readers are reminded of Padmore's explanation some fifteen years earlier of the two stages of revolution in African territories. Socialist Nkrumah was urged to deal with capitalist Danquah. The February 1948 riots in Accra signalled the beginning of Nkrumah's positive action campaign; at last one of the British African outposts seemed threatened. Padmore laid all responsibility for violence on the police, who, he said, had opened fire on innocents. The British public stood condemned for hypocrisy: it could raise a great deal of concern over the course of events in Czechoslovakia, yet remain utterly indifferent to death in Accra. A rally was held at Trafalgar Square and Padmore challenged the contention of the Colonial Under-Secretary, Rees Williams, that the Accra rioters were communists instead of nationalists.[32] The British Labour government, he wrote elsewhere, was more responsive to the needs of the United Africa Company than to the welfare of colonial peoples. Even so, the 'spectre of Pan-Africanism is haunting the "dark continent"'.[33] In this, he had the support of such reformist organisations as the LCP, which reported Accra affairs in full.*

Early in the year Padmore wrote to DuBois on the latter's eightieth birthday. The formality of their relations is suggested in the high-flown text, which sounds rather like a memorial tribute:

Unlike so many who, with shibboleths on their lips and self-interest in their hearts, have been seduced by money and office away from the struggle for the social emancipation and political freedom of our people, you have rejected the path of opportunism and clung steadfastly to your beliefs. Nor have you allowed those beliefs to remain sterile but have kept your mind active and alert to the point of bringing your ideas more into line with the current scene and temper of our people both in the

---

* Nkrumah's past already was in process of enlargement, for the LCP *Newsletter* referred to him as a 'professor of philosophy at Pennsylvania University'.

United States, in Africa and the West Indies, in whose hearts you have earned a place as a fighter for freedom and democratic justice.[34]

One wonders how a reply to this could be drafted.

In early summer, Padmore reported the proceedings of an international socialist conference, the Paris Congress of Peoples, which was held in the suburb of Puteaux on June 19–21. John McNair translated and some of his ILP colleagues, such as Brockway and Bob Edwards of the Chemical Workers Union, attended. One result was the formation of a permanent international committee. On it were Brockway, the ILP chairman David Gibson, a South African named Leon Szur—today in medical practice in London, but then newly arrived in the United Kingdom—and several Africans later important in their own countries, such as Yacoub Osman, Joe Appiah and Mbiyu Koinange.[35] This may be regarded as the last international socialist gathering to which Africans were attracted in significant numbers. Henceforth, they tended to organise their gatherings in the Manchester mode with fraternal delegates in attendance but control clearly in African hands. The cold war was well developed, the two greatest powers had simplified the issues, and the non-communist left seemed impotent. It was the final stage of any international orientation in African thinking. Henceforth, one would hear more and more about third forces, Afro-Asian blocs, neutralism and avoidance of Cold War entanglements.

8

Ghana: the Months of Power

PADMORE'S NEXT BOOK owed much to the ideas of an American diplomatic historian, Professor Lowell Ragatz, then of George Washington University, who argued that 'Britain has built and lost two great empires—in America and in India—but the prospects are that her third, in Africa, will be her greatest'.[1] F. A. Ridley had introduced readers of the *Socialist Leader* to this view, but already Padmore was persuaded that Ragatz was correct. He began work, at first calling the book *Africa and the Western Powers*, then *Britain's African Empire*, finally *Africa: Britain's Third Empire*. It was a good title and attracted a number of pre-publication orders, among them, in mid-January of the new year, one from Nkrumah in Accra.[2] Nkrumah's interest in the book differed, one presumes, from that displayed by another early enquirer, E. G. Sarsfield-Hall, who wrote to Dobson that he would 'be much obliged if you would tell me something about this gentleman and what qualifications he has for writing a magnum opus of this kind on Africa. I spent twenty-seven years in the administration in the Sudan where I was Governor of various Provinces and have been a member of the Royal African Society for many years but I do not seem to have ever heard of Mr George Padmore.'[3] Dobson replied as stiffly as he could to this magisterial enquiry: Padmore was 'a Colonial, a native of the West Indies, and has spent the greater part of his life in the cause of coloured people throughout the world'. He had 'sufficient qualifications for writing the book described in the leaflet which we sent you'.[4]

Padmore was living, as usual, close to the subsistence line. Dobson gave him a £25 advance, partly so he could pay Dorothy for typing. 'My good typist', Padmore wrote, 'has staged a "sit-down" strike. The charming girl has refused to do any more work until she gets paid.'[5] With luck, Makonnen and the PAF group might be persuaded to bring out a cheap paperback edition, for the book looked like being a money spinner. Makonnen, however, was not so keen unless 'the whole of the colonial market' was put in his hands, which Dobson thought out of the question.[6] All of this in any case was dependent upon the manuscript's actually being printed, and the apparently inevitable printers' delays made this seem unlikely. The publication date receded even farther into 1949, until in great distress Padmore wrote to his publisher:

So many people have written to me to express their disappoint-ment over the long delay of the copy of the book they ordered. I have tried to explain all difficulties and to assure them that we are really doing all that can be done to expedite matters. I have been most unfortunate with my books. The last was long in production but not as long as the present one. Since May 1948! By the time it comes out the Labour Party might have been a thing of the past. I wonder if you can urge on the printers. What is there to be done? I have spoken to Makonnen about the cheap edition but the man is not impressed. For we gave him the impression that the book would be out in the summer by the latest and he turned down an offer of a cheap edition of another book, expecting to handle mine. Now we don't even know when it will appear. He does not want to tie up his capital on a venture that shows no signs of materialising, and I can give him no definite assurance when he can have delivery. . . . An African recently wrote to Makonnen to order 500 copies of the first edition (one of his regular customers) but he returned the man's bank draft as he could get no definite information from us . . . my name will soon be mud in Africa. The natives will think I am trying to defraud them of their money. That is a common practice out there. People collect money for books which never appear. That is why I am so worried over its delay.[7]

By return post, Dobson's associate, James Gordon, assured the author that a new printer had been found and things were looking up. Padmore, ever ready for optimism, replied: 'I fully well appreciate the unforeseen difficulties which have arisen. It is these

damn Colonials who do not realise the many stages in book production. When they start writing for your firm you will then
realise what an angel I have been to deal with (laughter).'[8]

By the autumn things looked very good indeed. Padmore told
DuBois that the first edition was sold out before publication,
which should be at the year's end. 'Events have moved so fast that
I have had difficulty keeping the book up-to-date.' He dedicated
it to the professor and to the late Gold Coast leader, Casely-
Hayford, and he hoped that DuBois would 'write a short foreword
or preface to the American edition and recommend me to a
progressive publisher'. The book attempted 'to cover new ground
by reviewing the various nationalist and progressive movements
between the two world wars and since'. This was necessary, 'in
order to restate our independent anti-imperialist position, free of
all "entangling alliances" in the present East–West "cold war"'.[9]
The book appeared early in 1950 and the usual review copies were
sent to one Indian, six West Indian, twenty-two African and forty-
five British newspapers and periodicals.* It was well-received on
the left and execrated on the right. Ridley wrote: 'George Padmore
is a great African, whose contributions to the anti-imperialist
struggle are part of the world history of our times. If there is a
more dynamic critic of Imperialism in the British Empire', he
remarked pugnaciously, 'I do not know his name or whereabouts.'[10]

Perhaps because Ridley was right, the book was banned immediately in Kenya, and a month later the Gold Coast government
followed suit. In May, a nervous book dealer wrote from Bathurst
that its circulation was also prohibited in Gambia. 'I am a member
of this Government', the poor man entreated, 'and do not wish to
be complicated with matters of this nature leading into trouble or
suspicion. I therefore in the circumstances earnestly request you

---

* Padmore, despite his contacts with WASU and persons such as
Kenyatta, who had been a Kikuyu language informant at the School of
Oriental and African Studies of London University, had no entry into the
British academic world. When the book was published, Dobson remarked
(in a letter, February 6, 1950) that he understood the author was going
to have posters displayed at the university, to which Padmore replied
(on February 8): 'I am afraid I am in no position to arrange a poster at
the School of Oriental and African Studies, so this must be for you to do,
if you can.' One cannot help feeling that both the university and Padmore
might have benefited from the encounter.

to cancel the order forthwith and return my money.'[11] Azikiwe, on the other hand, explained that 'we have been given assurance of some sort that there is no prospect at the present to ban it' in Nigeria, and advised Dobson to consign the stipulated 5,000 copies to his African Book Company Limited of Lagos.[12] So much for the vagaries of colonial censorship. This notoriety, naturally, was good for sales. Padmore, encouraged by the book's reputation, wrote to DuBois that already he was at work on another. 'My last had a tremendous success', though he still wanted the Doctor's help in finding an American publisher. This could not be done, however, as American hysteria in the early months of the Korean War made it almost impossible for anything radical to be published. DuBois himself lacked an outlet at the time.[13] Indeed, soon afterwards, DuBois became the object of considerable attention from the American government, and Padmore did what he could to protest against the indictment of the Peace Information Center. 'The case aroused enormous sympathy and indignation and while I was on the Gold Coast', Padmore said after his first trip there, 'I spoke about it at some of my meetings and resolutions were sent to the American consul.'[14]

By the end of the year, a second edition was being printed and Fenner Brockway, newly returned to the House of Commons, was persuaded to intervene with the Colonial Secretary, James Griffiths. Surely, Brockway wrote, Griffiths must agree that the work was scholarly. Its suppression was both contrary to the British way of doing things and counter-productive: 'traders are importing the book and selling it at double price. As frequently happens, the ban is only increasing the interest of the book and is at the same time arousing prejudice against the British authorities.' Besides, the Colonial Secretary himself had expressed an interest in reading the book. For the second edition, Brockway added, Padmore was writing a preface critical of the ban. 'He would greatly prefer not to do so and is hoping that I may be able to assure him that the ban will be lifted. He would then of course amend his preface so as to express his appreciation of this. I appreciate', he added somewhat lamely, 'that this sounds a little like a threat or a bargain, but it is not intended in that spirit at all. I am finding among colonial representatives a real desire to be acting with us for their freedom and this is the spirit in which George

Padmore approached me.'[15] Brockway's state of mind was interesting, to be sure, but, if he rightly interpreted, Padmore's also raises many questions. One cannot help but feel that Brockway misconstrued.

While all this was taking place, Padmore had continued his journalistic career. On a number of occasions in 1948, he was in Paris, mostly reporting United Nations news for the Negro press. Paris, he often remarked to Dobson, offered a big market for his books, if only they could be translated reputably. Parisian publishers 'want to talk business as the colonial question is very topical'. The French, incredibly enough, were even less inclined to divest themselves of empire than the British. They have not been able to comprehend, he wrote apropos of Madagascar, that 'the French Union cannot be built on the cemetery, hatred and coercion'.[16] From Paris he also apprised DuBois of the four-day conference of October 1949 which had been held in London to express disappointment with the Labour government's reluctance to encourage West African freedom. The meeting was chaired by Brockway and convened by the Congress of Peoples Against Imperialism, at Denison House in the Vauxhall Bridge Road. There they decided to change their unwieldy name to the British Centre for Colonial Freedom, which somehow seemed more specific. But, this too was amended in the following March, when they became the Congress for Colonial Freedom, a title adopted at their April meeting at the Waldorf Hotel. Nevertheless, they soon became known as the Movement for Colonial Freedom (MCF).[17]

'Quite a number of African delegates attended' these sessions, Padmore told DuBois, 'among them Dr Azikiwe, the leader of the Nigerian National Council, and Yosuf Osman, the assistant secretary of the Umma Party of Sudan. I have been in Paris carrying on discussions with French friends [presumably Daniel Guerin]. Dr Azikiwe joins me in a few days before returning to Africa. We are trying to get him to take the initiative in preparing the 6th Congress.' This was the last occasion on which Padmore expressed any confidence in Azikiwe's supra-Nigerian orientation. There were handicaps, he continued, as 'the African Nationalist and Anti-Imperialist Movements are faced with the difficult problem of being branded "Communists" and "Moscow Agents" by the British, even the Labour Party. This has resulted in splits in the camp and in weakening the Pan-African Front. However, without identifying ourselves openly with either the Anglo-Saxon or Russian power blocs, we are keeping the banner of Pan-Africanism firmly in our hands, co-operating with those who support our 5th Congress Programme and ignoring the others.' Readers will note this early statement of the modern African credo.[18]

Throughout, Padmore also maintained his interest in the annual ILP Summer Schools. In 1950 he spoke on the topic "Is Imperialism dead?" at the George Hotel in Bangor, with the negative findings one might expect.[19] But in the following year, for the first time since 1937 except for those occasions when he was too ill to attend, Padmore had to cancel his appearance. Though he was listed to speak at the Kingsmoor School in Derbyshire,[20] he was in fact in Lagos covering the situation created by the new MacPherson–Foot Constitution. Azikiwe, he wrote ominously in July,[21] could emerge as a truly national figure in the Nkrumah sense only if tribalism were eliminated.*

He had come to Nigeria by way of the Gold Coast, to which he had been invited by that confident political prisoner, Nkrumah, who was certain the Convention Peoples' Party (CPP) would win the February 1951 elections and who wanted Padmore to chronicle the remarkable history of postwar events. Padmore was apt for the task, as this letter of January 8, 1951, to DuBois illustrates:

> The elan in the Gold Coast is high and the determination of the people as of the CPP to get dominion status as quickly as possible is unflagging. I can assure you that there is absolutely no truth in the information you have received about the lack of integrity of the CPP leaders. The statement you quote is a travesty of the truth. . . . While I do not wish to enquire of you as to your informants, I can guess the sources of these slanderous statements: Dr Armattoe and Dr Danquah. . . . Just at this moment they are girding their forces for the local government elections which will take place in April, and which will give them instruments of administration not merely at the apex but throughout the

---

* Next year he made up for his previous summer's absence by speaking at the ILP Summer School at Wortley Hall, Sheffield. John McNair recorded in his diary that on Friday, August 15, 'Padmore spoke magnificently, once again reminding them that his grandfather was a slave'. (Letter, McNair to author, September 8, 1964.)

country. There has been a complete break down of the 'native' administration through an almost wholesale attack upon the 'stools', which had to be stemmed in order not to create a complete anarchy in government and a situation which might have held in it something of disaster.[22]

Readers of Dennis Austin's *Politics in Ghana* might consider this biased.

However, Nkrumah had been correct in his expectations. In August, Padmore was invited back to Accra to witness Nkrumah's installation as Leader of Government Business at the reopening of the Legislative Council.[23] He reported enthusiastically about the CPP's plans for compulsory free primary education and economic expansion, and worried over the chieftainship crisis. He did not wish to see chiefs eliminated, provided they recognised where power lay in the new state, for they lent tone and cohesiveness in tribal circumstances.[24]

Padmore returned to London early in October,* and, while continuing to write for the press, set to work on another book. The first fruits of this new venture appeared in the March 1952 issue of *The Crisis* as "Bloodless Revolution in the Gold Coast". It was a review of modern Gold Coast history in the Whig tradition of historiography: all was but a prelude to the advent of Nkrumah and the good times. Nkrumah's West African National Secretariat was linked to the original West African National Congress, despite a seventeen-year hiatus, and Gold Coast progress was made a function of Nkrumah's character. This became a fixed point of

---

* At the end of September, the then editor of the *Socialist Leader*, George Stone, wrote somewhat mysteriously that Padmore was 'leaving Europe in a few weeks time to take his place as leader of the Socialist and Democratic forces in the West Indies'. While Dorothy Pizer did travel to the islands then, I have no evidence that Padmore also contemplated this course. There is some evidence to suggest that he occasionally thought about returning to the United States—at least when Roi Ottley saw him in this period he thought Padmore regarded London as a place of 'unhappy and forlorn exile' (*No Green Pastures*, page 68), and he had asked DuBois if he thought any American foundation would subsidise him: 'How can I get a fellowship to continue my work? Do you think Dr Johnson of Fisk would help? My life has been very much like yours— work but no money.' (Letter from Paris, October 31, 1949.) But there is nothing that hints at a return to the Caribbean.

faith, which put some of Padmore's admirers rather out of sorts during his remaining seven years of life. The article foreshadowed the book. This latest volume, Padmore told his publisher, would be dedicated to Nkrumah. He had not worked out the title yet— probably it would be something like that of *The Crisis* article—but at the moment he was so busy 'running errands between here and the continent' for the Gold Coast leader that he had no time to think.[25] Nevertheless, the book took form. It would be a good idea to put his photo on the dust jacket in the Penguin fashion, he told Dobson. Africans were always after photos and did not realise that authors were not like film stars, with endless publicity pictures to hand out. In this way, provided they bought the book, 'Africans can cut me out as their "stick-up boy" '. It might be useful to put Nkrumah's photo in the frontispiece, too, he added.[26]

Through March 1953 he plugged away, on one occasion changing a passage about a certain colonial official because of Dobson's fear that it was actionable,[27] and in late spring *The Gold Coast Revolution* finally was printed. Tom Colyer reviewed it for the ILP newspaper on June 20. He approved Padmore's depiction of Nkrumah as the embodiment of the hopes which international socialists had for renascent Africa and claimed that the Gold Coast colony had gone down a road all Africa would follow. Understandably, the book did well in West Africa. Padmore received a shilling a copy on those sold to Nkrumah's CPP, and was urged to write another specifically for the party. This seemed a good idea, he told Dobson, and probably it would be ready 'early in 1955 as Nkrumah is planning to call a Pan-African Congress and needs the book in advance for publicity purposes. The subject deals with "Black Zionism, Pan-Africanism and Communism".'[28] This was an advance notice for his last and most famous work, *Pan-Africanism or Communism?*.

But, apart from Colyer, the critics were hostile. Left establishmentarians considered that Padmore had written a work disfigured with 'many distortions and prejudices'.[29] The most acerbic review came once again from the pen of a WASU member (possibly W. A. N. Adumua-Bossman):

There is no need for us to vindicate the claim of George Padmore to be one of the outstanding historians of the African nationalist background. His researches into, and findings about, the social background of the political leaders, their motives and the limits of their political methods, have had some influence on African political thinking and discussion. In the past some of his books have shown some refreshing respect for facts which most books written by British historians have hopelessly lacked. . . . George Padmore was, therefore, honoured when he was invited to the Gold Coast in 1951 by the Convention Peoples Party to view this exciting phenomenon at first hand. But Padmore's enthusiasm for the part played by his hosts has proved too much for his judgment and his assessment of the situation. No one can read the book without the immediate feeling of Padmore's determination *not* to appear to be too honest and as open-minded as any reasonable person can be, when he discusses a subject so deeply embedded in passionate and fundamental emotions. The language he uses to describe the political opponents of the CPP can be described as uncouth; his opinion of Nkrumah borders on religious veneration—no adjective is good enough to describe the absolute infallibility of Nkrumah. Some of his facts are incorrect, and others have been falsified in different parts of the book to justify different arguments.[30]

This was strong, but the reviewer had been stung by Padmore's assumption that a favourable environment explained pre-war nationalist movements, while 'post-war nationalist achievement was due to the supreme revolutionary genius of Kwame Nkrumah'. Ironically, Padmore was accused of failing 'to appreciate, must less to mention, the effect of the Russian Revolution on imperialist actions'. Nevertheless, Padmore's critic made several shrewd points. The executive of the CPP, he remarked, seemed as much a part of the old professional class as the now-maligned former leaders. To talk about a revolution of the left in the Gold Coast 'can only result in that confusion of ideas which makes men cease to understand one another's thoughts'. Moreover, Padmore did not make it sufficiently clear that while 'in pre-war years an African politician had to convince men of the *necessity* for action, in post-war years that necessity was conceded, and political agitation becomes a discussion of the form of action'. This essay was written during the feverish second Gold Coast general election, that prelude to freedom from British rule, which partly accounts for its severity.[31] Still, it struck out at those tendencies in Padmore's thought which most distressed many of his former comrades.

Late in the year Padmore tried, through Guerin, to develop a French outlet for his articles. Several which he had sent an Indian journalist in Paris appeared unacceptable. It was, he noted, 'very difficult to place such things in France'. Guerin suggested some possibilities, but nothing came of them. 'The French', Padmore generalised, 'are much less businesslike than the Anglo-Saxons. They work faster here and still faster in the USA.' He was 'rather run-down and extremely tired and nervous', according to Dorothy, who asked if they might stay at Guerin's flat for the holidays. He had addressed rallies for all manner of colonial, especially African, causes (in September it had been the Awolowo–Azikiwe delegation from Nigeria and representatives of the proscribed Kenya African Union), and written lengthy and immensely informative articles about events in Uganda and British Guiana; in the latter case he again demonstrated that his readers were better served than were devotees of the capitalist daily press. While the Anglo-American papers laboured away at the sinister associations of the Jagan family, Padmore deftly sketched the racial and economic realities of that South American limbo. Surprisingly, his information on Kenya was not so impressive. The region was 'tightly closed and there is severe restriction on news and information', he wrote to DuBois. 'Mail is always watched from the original sources, censorship of news presents the same difficulty indirectly.'[32] His principal Kenya contact after Kenyatta's imprisonment was Mbiyu Koinange.[33]

Padmore apparently managed to scrape up some money, because on December 13 they flew to Paris. 'I am very busy', he told Guerin, 'bursting with ideas for books but can find no time to get them down as I must keep up with my journalism—hard day to day grinding work to meet my expenses.'[34] However, he was not too busy to confer with a Bahanda delegation which had come to London to protest against their Kabaka's exile. He described the meeting in a letter to DuBois, and added: 'Pan-Africanism on the march . . . congrats on Stalin Peace Prize.'[35]

A week before going on vacation, Padmore missed what technically qualified as the sixth Pan-African Congress, which Nkrumah convened in Kumasi on the weekend of December 7 and 8. Few attended, and Padmore never mentioned it—sure proof of its obscurity—but Azikiwe and H. O. Davies from Nigeria, some conferees from francophone countries and W. F. Conton of Sierra Leone did meet with Nkrumah* to consider 'ways of and means of speeding up the liberation of Africa and establishing a strong West African Federation'.[36]

While on holiday, Padmore was named in the *Report of the Commission of Enquiry into Mr Braimah's Resignation and Allegations Arising Therefrom* (Korsah Report); for the first time since his break with the Comintern he was accused of corruption. According to testimony which the Gold Coast commission accepted, Padmore had negotiated a low-cost housing contract in Ghana for a Dutch firm, which had paid him five per cent of the winning bid, half of which Padmore in turn had offered to the CPP. The original Reuters despatch which *The Times* printed gave no source, but subsequently the informant was identified as Braimah's attorney, Koi Larbi.[37] Padmore stiffly denied the allegation and was told by the commissioners that there was no need to go into the matter, as it was subsidiary and mentioned only in passing. This naturally did not satisfy Padmore, who instructed the editor of the Gold Coast *Daily Graphic* to print a challenge to anyone willing to repeat the charge. His entire gain from a brief visit to that colony in 1951, he wrote, had been a £50 collection offered by the CPP. The allegation was forgotten.[38]

This distasteful occurrence did not prevent him from returning to Africa, for in May he told Dobson that he was 'planning to leave for the Gold Coast to report on the forthcoming election' and would like to straighten out his royalties account. 'I might', he added, 'have a new book for you on my return.'[39] While away, he despatched to the *Socialist Leader* one of his increasingly adulatory articles about Nkrumah, who was beginning to assume legendary proportions. Padmore now appeared to be writing about an institution and he attributed a significance to Gold Coast events which was completely out of proportion to that colony's size and prospects. His American readers, too, were subjected to regular

---

* Students of Nkrumah's changing image will note that by 1953 he rarely was called a Gold Coaster, often not even a West African, but rather frequently was designated simply an African.

instalments of the Nkrumah legend. Readers of *The Crisis* for January 1955 were told that the modification of the Gold Coast constitution was a tribute to Nkrumah's popularity, which represented 'a hope and inspiration to Africans everywhere', and cautioned that the British and their African stooges nevertheless continued to plan the subversion of CPP programmes. These two themes were dominant in Padmore's writings from that time, as a letter to DuBois indicates:

> I have asked the Minister of State to send you all recent reports on the Gold Coast Industrial Revolution as I get the impression that you are fed upon all the slanders, rumours and misrepresentation from the enemy (chiefs, tribalist separatists like the Ashanti traditionalists who want to go back to the days of human sacrifice and slave trade) plus the British capitalist interests out to smash the cocoa marketing State control monopoly which Nkrumah adopted out of the Russian book and applied to local conditions. Thus all the talk about 'black dictatorship and Nkrumah introducing Communism'. Who says so? Discredited politicians like Dr Danquah,* and aspiring African capitalist elements. Unfortunately, the British Communists are playing the same game, and as a result, the courts here recently awarded the UAC £5,000 damages against the London *Daily Worker* for accusing them of exploiting the farmers. Whereas in fact, the UAC is out of the export business since Nkrumah set up the Cocoa Marketing Board. The *DW* was still thinking of the days when Archie Nichoi [Ashie Nikoi, see *Colonial and Coloured Unity*] poured out his heart at the Pan-African Congress. Those days are over. The revolution is on the march.[40]

Nkrumah's autobiography, he later wrote in *The Crisis* (April 1957), would 'do for the Negro liberation movements what Tom Paine's *Common Sense* did for the Americans in their most difficult period of revolt against British colonialism'. His assessment of the

---

* Padmore, I believe, met Danquah in 1930. 'I never thought much of him', he wrote in 1932. 'I think fellows like him would be a hundred times more useful . . . had they never gone abroad and imbibed the stupid ideology of the alien ruling class.' (Letter to Kobina Sekyi, July 9, 1932, quoted in Samuel Rohdie's interesting, though unfair, article, "The Gold Coast Aborigines Abroad", *Journal of African History*, Vol. VI, No. 3, 1965.)

book and his view of eighteenth-century British history both seem distorted.

In mid-June he returned to London and shortly thereafter was asked by Guerin to find rooms and a summer job for a young French socialist. In his somewhat perfunctory reply Padmore remarked that the communists had ruined his French prospects. Some months before he had sent a copy of *The Gold Coast Revolution* to Jeanson of Editions du Seuil, hoping to interest him in a French language version, but had heard nothing. 'It seems that you are the only Frenchman who deals with correspondence. Perhaps it is your long Anglo-Saxon contacts (laughter).' Only now he learned by way of his Indian journalist friend there that Jeanson's translator 'turned out to be a Communist and he sabotaged it with Editions du Seuil. . . . It seems that the C P have their agents everywhere in France.' In his usual way he reminded Guerin of Gallic frailty. That sort of thing 'could not happen here' he assured him. Not that Padmore cared all that much, but he had thought the French more worldly. He now concluded that the French were far less likely to get out of their portion of Togo than were the British, for 'your colonialists seem to learn nothing and forget nothing. They hold on to every little bit of foreign land like typical peasants.' Throughout his life, Padmore displayed a rather trying francophobia, which he contradictorily coupled with the assertion that race relations were more amicable in French territories.

Meanwhile, his new book, the one tentatively promised to Dobson, took shape. 'I am trying', he wrote to Guerin, 'to finish the first draft of a book on "Black Zionism", in which I am recording the history of the Garvey "Back to Africa Movement", Pan-Africanism and Communism. . . . I am covering new ground on the Negro political problem.'[41] He amplified his remarks in a letter to DuBois:

You will be pleased to hear that in order to let the younger generation know of your contributions to Africa's freedom, I have been commissioned to do a book on the Pan-African Congress which I hope to have published by the middle of 1955. Dr Nkrumah is keen on it as he plans to convene a sixth* Pan-

* Even here Padmore refused to credit the Kumasi conference.

African Congress on the Gold Coast as soon as independence is formally declared. We cannot do it before as we don't want to create undue alarm before we have full power in our hands. All goes well there despite last minute attempts by the imperialists to incite tribalism to disrupt the national united front. The recent victory of Dr Azikiwe's NCNC in Nigeria is a blow against tribalism and if he plays his hands correctly we hope to consolidate a united Nigerian front. It is a skilful game of manoeuvring and we cannot afford at this stage of the struggle to give the imperialists any excuse to intervene as in British Guiana. . . . Our victory in Uganda is now assured. It will move forward as an African State and detached from any association with Kenya, where the struggle goes on. If our people hold out for another year, the whites will have to quit. It is a bloody battle but unavoidable.* So was Haiti. Believe me dear Doctor, no force on earth can now hold back the forward march of Africa. Without the outside support of the Tories here and the US the writing would be clear for all to see, that Africa will soon take her place among the free nations. It is a great pity that Afro-American newspapers are not giving the struggle the publicity that it deserves. Even the *Courier* and *Defender* that at one time carried my despatches are no longer interested. I presume they feel that they have nothing in Africa. How unlike the Jews in their support of Israel.[42]

Though he was impatient with French ways, Padmore longed for a Paris holiday. He told Guerin that he needed 'a change of intellectual air' and hoped to find the money for a visit as soon as the first draft was done. Dorothy would not be with him, as she was to go to the Gold Coast in July for the first visit to what was to be her final home. In the meantime, Padmore busied himself with a meeting convened to hear Fenner Brockway report on his recent trip to Tunis and with the preparation, in collaboration with Douglas Rogers of the MCF, of a special issue of the Indian magazine *United Asia*, which was scheduled to come out at the time of the

---

* Padmore was first (in *The Crisis*, May 1954) among those who argued that the Mau Mau atrocities served a useful purpose if they forced a lethargic parliament to recognise the basis and extent of African dissatisfaction. He was the intellectual progenitor of such revisionist historians as J. Kariuki, whose *Mau Mau Detainee*, Oxford 1963, echoes this view.

imminent Bandung Conference of Afro-Asian Peoples. (Padmore's own contribution was a valuable essay on Gold Coast nationalism.) He asked Guerin to get up an article on Madagascar, a simple one 'as Asians don't even know where Madagascar is, much less what happened there', he added.[43] Padmore had learned of Madagascar, apart from books, through his friend André Ramanankoto, a young Malagasy student who translated French for him. Chandler, Padmore's Swedish acquaintance, recalls that he chanced to be in the offices of the MCF at the same time as Ramanankoto. 'I told him I was interested in African history, so he gave me a lot of history about Madagascar and said "If you want to know about Africa, the expert is George Padmore. Why don't you go and see him?" So I did.' Chandler remembers two points from this meeting vividly: Padmore indignantly beat down the notion that Blyden was not the West Indian *non pareil*, and equally strenuously insisted that Nkrumah was cast from the same heroic mould.[44]

Busy as he was, his manuscript was completed before the end of the year. With luck, he estimated it would be out in four months; at least, it had been accepted for April publication. He still had one chapter to revise, and this he did while at last on his Paris holiday that Christmas. On December 23, Dorothy and he flew over and once more stayed at Guerin's flat. 'We spend much of the time admiring the passing traffic on the river', she remarked in her bread and butter note. Padmore needed 'a holiday after a very hard year's work', though his idea of rest was somewhat singular. 'I shall spend my last days completing a chapter in my book', he told Guerin in a note reminding him about that Madagascar article. 'The Asian–African Conference takes place in April and we must bring out the issue of *United Asia* in time.'[45] Dorothy had to be back at work after New Year's Day, but Padmore stayed on in Paris till January 7. They had had Christmas dinner with the Richard Wrights* and some unspecified Vietnamese, but otherwise seem to have kept to themselves.

* Wright's *Black Power* (Harper, New York 1954) struck him as 'a very good book indeed', and he urged Guerin to buy it. This is interesting, for the American novelist had tried but failed to identify with the peoples of his ancestral continent. DuBois did not like the book, which, surprisingly, Padmore did not anticipate. Padmore assured DuBois (in a letter, December 10, 1954) that Wright had caught 'the challenge of the *barefoot*

The book still commanded attention. Padmore took another three-week holiday in Paris the following July (Dorothy again commented on the river boats, which she found extremely soothing), but by August was hard at work again. 'Don't forget to write about the Garvey photo—United Press Agency, New York', he admonished Dobson's man. 'Tell them it is the one with the African "Emperor" dressed up in his marshal's uniform and cock-hat with plumes and peacock feathers.'[46] By October he was reading page proofs and Dorothy had embarked upon an index, 'always a most thankless task', as she said. On November 16 she again wrote to Guerin that she was 'busy working on the horrible index for G's book; otherwise, the page proofs have been returned to the printer, and it should be out now within a few weeks'. Those familiar with the book will know what a monumental job she did, for the index runs to $10\frac{1}{2}$ pages of fine print.

Padmore had secured Richard Wright's agreement to contribute a foreword, and it looked as though both American and French editions also would be printed. The Egyptian Ministry of Information had approached him regarding an Arabic edition of *Africa: Britain's Third Empire*, and he believed that *The Gold Coast Revolution* and his latest work might interest them even more. He told Dobson he wanted an agreement before his works were pirated, though without an agent in Cairo the piracy might go undetected.[47] Wright's foreword turned out to be a bit tricky for inclusion in the colonial edition. Padmore told Dobson on March 6 that 'as far as I am concerned it can be used in both the English and American editions—but not the Colonial. I think Wright certainly let himself go. His attitude is: plague on both East and West. But he is honest and I respect him for that.'

Meanwhile, the book, which had been 'going through the press' in January, was delayed by another labour dispute during that bitterly cold February of 1956. 'At the moment', he wrote to Guerin, 'we are faced with a wave of strikes in the printing industry . . . books already in press are being held-up. Mine should have been out in March and now it has been put back to May and

---

masses against the *black aristocracy and middle class*' (thus antedating the much commended Frantz Fanon), but DuBois remained unconvinced (letter to Padmore, December 25, 1954). Perhaps it all sounded too much like Garvey for him to enjoy it.

even that depends upon whether the strike is settled', he added disconsolately. He was too optimistic, for in June he had not completed the index, he worried over the list of those to receive complimentary copies and was distracted by the imminent Gold Coast elections. Then he went down with a painful bladder infection. Perhaps, he told Guerin, the book would be out that month; certainly, there was too much to do for the illness to be convenient. He had, for instance, to marshal support for those Frenchmen who had been imprisoned for opposition to the Algerian war.[48] In this, he was quite successful, but then, as he later wrote acidly to Guerin: 'The British are always ready to hear colonials other than theirs.'[49]

Dorothy reported in July that Padmore was up and about, though tired, and 'anxiously awaiting the outcome of the Gold Coast elections. It seems ages even to Wednesday, when the results are through, and if the accounts we have been receiving are any indication, Nkrumah should be returned with a good over-all majority. The British imperialists, however, are up to their tricks and will pull a "fast one" if they possibly can. But the temper of the people is pitched high and they will have independence this year by one means or another.'[50] Polls were opened on the following day and by evening it was apparent that the CPP had at least retained power. Soon, returns indicated that even in Ashanti, where opposition was violent, Nkrumah candidates had done better than expected. In the event, the CPP won 71 of the 104 seats in the Gold Coast Legislature. Within a fortnight they called for independence, and on September 18 Lennox-Boyd, the Secretary of State for the Colonies, announced that the British government would ask parliament to honour the demand on the following March 6. Dorothy's estimate of her countrymen's intentions was incorrect.[51]

She was loyal, however, to Padmore's view that there could be no objectivity concerning colonialism—one might as well be dispassionate about fascism. He had written to Guerin:

> I distrust people who talk to me about objectivity and despise people who run with the hares and hunt with the hounds. It makes me angry when I hear one author condemning the work of another on the spurious ground of 'objectivity'. Leave that to

The Times and God! . . . No nationalist can be objective where
the fate of his country's freedom is involved. The trouble with
most British people is: they have not had any foreigners sitting
on their necks since the Danes and the Normans. So they are
the only people who make a fetish of 'objectivity', except when
Napoleon and Hitler were threatening to 'visit' them and turn
them into 'natives'—as conquered people are called. I presume
Miss Lucy [generic for the white madam] should be 'objective'
and take her kicks![52]

The bitterness of his tone, most unusual in Padmore's utterances,
tends to distract one's attention away from his main point: no help
could be expected from the British when it came to dismantling
their empire. 'We have to mobilize the Afro-Asian powers to
watch John Bull and our so-called socialists.'[53] They seemed to
think that 'the simple-minded natives just look to the Labour
Party for salvation, etc., etc. All nonsense! . . . Talking about the
"cult of the individual" ', he remarked angrily to Dobson's wife,
'Stalin and his cronies have nothing on the Labour careerists and
opportunists. They must think we are "mugs", as the Americans
say.'[54]

By now a new danger, one far more insidious than earlier kinds,
had presented itself. Padmore was among the first to identify
neocolonialism, the condition so widely deplored in later years by
his friend Nkrumah. There was a likelihood, Padmore and Guerin
agreed early in 1956, that any lessening of cold war tensions would
damage the cause of colonial advancement. As he put it in his last
book: 'If the East and West settle their differences, the Russians
will liquidate the Cominform and the British Communists will
again desert their present "allies for freedom", as the colonials are
now flatteringly called.'[55] Whereas, earlier, he had worried that
America's fear of Russia would lead her to ignore colonial questions
in her search for allies, now he seemed to argue that the removal of
the Russian threat would induce a corresponding indifference to
colonialism in the Americans. Just as contradictorily, he argued
that any effort to stifle nationalism would drive Africans into
the communist camp.

Padmore was not well for most of the summer of 1956. Once
again he begged off his ILP Summer School commitment. He

had intended to speak on "Apartheid, Bantu Nationalism and Communism", but, despite the new general secretary's description of Padmore as a first-flight orator, a 'fighter for colonial freedom, indomitable and untiring', he was exhausted and, on July 30, went into hospital. He had been confined to bed in June 'with a severe chill on the bladder, which [was] affected by urination, and has been the cause of intense pain which is gradually improving', he told Guerin.[56] Dr Clarke recommended a warm climate, but, without French currency, there was nothing to be done; Padmore stayed home, hoping at least for another Parisian Christmas. But, though Guerin again offered his flat, that also fell through. Nor was he able to attend the African writers' congress sponsored by *Présence Africaine* at the Sorbonne that September, though he had been one of the principal authors invited. However, he preserved a cheerful exterior. 'All is well with me', he told Dobson, 'except that as soon as I work for money it slips out of my hand.'[57]

This was not precisely the case, for finally, on Monday, August 20, *Pan-Africanism or Communism?* appeared. Advance sales were good. Dobson earlier had told Padmore that three French firms were after the book for translation, and Padmore wrote to Guerin that 'the Americans have already taken it and 5,000 copies have been sold in Africa already'.[58] An edition was issued simultaneously for the Zik Press in Nigeria. Azikiwe did not want his own imprint on it (perhaps because of the caustic way in which Zik's affiliation to Moral Rearmament was handled in the book, perhaps because it was likely to be banned), Richard Wright's strong preface was omitted and the title was changed to the somewhat misleading but for Africans more attractively simple *Pan-Africanism.*[59] Padmore sent off review and presentation copies to persons such as Brockway and DuBois and the editors of journals ranging from *The Crisis* to *Présence Africaine*, from Norway to Georgia, from India to the West Indies, from London to Cape Town. Only fourteen of them were not personal friends,[60] some indication of the extent of his acquaintance and influence.

His friend Guerin also was ill, but contrived to write to Padmore from a Swiss clinic, congratulating him on his book. 'I learned very much from it and I admire your knowledge, your talent, combined with the passion of the militant.' Still, he thought, there were troublesome portions. The French sections, for a start, were badly mis-spelled. Padmore agreed at once, though he asked if Guerin had any notion of the way that English printers treated foreign names. 'What they cannot make out, they just invent and the more you correct, the more mistakes appear. Checking up on my proofs I discovered that many of the names were correctly spelt but the printers paid no respect to them.' And Guerin pointed out that there were Frenchmen, himself included, who might have been named in the list of 'premature pro-Africans' who appeared on page 365. Padmore assured him that this would be amended in the second edition (which never appeared).

Guerin's principal complaint had more substance: Padmore was provincially English. He might have mentioned the anti-colonial league which Count Savorgnan de Brazza's secretary in the Congo, Felicien Challaye, founded in Paris in 1906. He should have given more credit to Emile Faure. The French were not nearly as free of racist attitudes as Padmore said, nor did they get along with educated Africans much better than the British did. Also, 'In my opinion you are too eulogistic towards the Commonwealth. And when you, very correctly, denounce the "bogus and fraudulent device to maintain French domination", why do you forget the device of the fetichist British Queen, used in order to keep together the several parts of the Commonwealth?' Moreover, Padmore was naïve in a racist way. It might be true that Belgium lived well off the Congo, as Padmore said on page 219, if by that he meant a small group of capitalists, but it was not true of 'the proletarians, for example the miners. The life in the Belgian coalfields is horrible.'

But, finally, Guerin's objections came to this: Padmore was anti-communist in a doctrinal way.

I am afraid that you mix-up communism (or Marxism) with Stalinism, and also that sometimes your justified hate against Stalinism makes you too indulgent towards the *reactionary* anti-communist forces. . . . You use the words 'doctrinaire Marxism' (as pp. 149 and 339) without explaining the difference between 'doctrinaire' Marxism and Marxism. You give the impression (because of too vague definitions) to contradict yourself when you write on p. 337 that communism is meeting with stubborn resistance from the adherents of pan-Africanism and when you somewhere else write that many of the young

Negro intellectuals in Britain held 'Marxist views' (p. 147) and that both Garveyism and pan-Africanism 'resemble Marxism' (p. 329). Then you *do homage* to communism when you observe that many of the present day students come from artisan families and peasant communities and are, therefore, more responsive to communist propaganda than those connected with the chieftain caste, etc. (p. 329). This means that there is a class struggle and that the communists are on the good side of the fence, the side of the poor. But, if so, why do you seem *to be delighted* when you say that most of these students on returning home revert to bourgeois nationalists, reactionary at fifty (p. 330)? And how can the reader understand why communism is your enemy number 1 when you admit (on p. 372) that *tribalism and not communism* is the immediate threat, the present menace. Sometimes you are very much anti-communist and sometimes you behave like a genuine Marxist. . . . Finally, my dear George, I am a little worried about a 'pan-Africanism' which would be an empty slogan without much more contents than anti-communism. . . . How to go beyond bourgeois nationalism? The answer is *socialism, marxism, communism*, but not the caricature of marxism and communism offered by Stalin and his agents. Why don't you say that clearly?[61]

Padmore responded to this lengthy charge a week later, obviously annoyed at what he termed Guerin's 'kind and constructive letter'.

I am afraid that you have entirely misunderstood the argument. There is no question of anti-communism. . . . As even *The Times* review understood, my author's defence was simple: after all, I cannot write history like the Stalinist—leave out the names of people because I disapprove of their politics. His [Diagne's] name was only mentioned in the historical context of having facilitated DuBois in holding his first Pan-African Congress. Diagne was never a pillar of pan-Africanism. That is made quite clear. A Stalinist would have simply dropped his name as they do that of Trotsky in their history books and just say: a certain African Deputy helped DuBois, etc., etc. That would be dishonest. In the same way Eboué's name appears. But he did exist and played a certain role like other Frenchmen —white and black—in recent history.

Padmore's laudatory comments about Moral Rearmament, which the Frenchman considered to be a 'well subsidised instrument of the State Department', dismayed Guerin as well. Padmore readily admitted that he had praised 'the biggest joke of all', the body 'used by Africans to get passports to come out of their prisons. . . . There is a good reason why I mentioned them in my book. By attacking them in a subtle way they are now on the defensive and have to buy copies of my book to prove that they are anti-red and instead of the book being banned in the colonies, the authorities allow it to be read by Africans who would otherwise be jailed for possessing a copy. We know the mentality of our rulers and how to kill a dog without choking it.'[62]*

At winter's end in 1957, Padmore was one of the celebrities invited to attend the Ghanaian independence ceremonies. Dr Clarke and Professor Arthur Lewis were the other prominent West Indians invited out to Accra for the March 6 ceremonies. Padmore, said Hugh Smythe in *The Crisis* for that April, 'is the silent hero of Ghana and a figure venerated and respected throughout black Africa', and went on to quote some fervid lines from Wright's foreword in *Pan-Africanism or Communism?*. But the cosmopolite did not fit easily into the West African scene. He 'did not look very convincing to me in the kente cloth robe he was affecting', recalls another of the guests, his former teacher, Dr Ralph Bunche.[63]

Dorothy had to return to London early in April, but George stayed on to cover for the *Socialist Leader* the elections in Freetown.[64] He also unsuccessfully tried to recover two outstanding accounts from Ghanaian book sellers who still owed Dobson nearly a thousand pounds.[65] There is little doubt that he very much wanted to remain in Ghana. According to Dorothy Abrahams, Padmore needed a job and was growing apprehensive for the future. It was her impression that his relations with Dorothy Pizer were strained, that indeed there had been some talk of her leaving him. None of this comes through in the Pizer–Guerin letters.

* Rohdie, in *Journal of African History*, Vol. VI, No. 3, 1965, p. 391, contends that Padmore's 'book is filled with similar innuendoes and cheap anti-communist slurs. He wrote it at the height of the cold war and is anxious to prove his own disillusion and change of heart. . . . The issues of the 1930s are seen in a very different light by him in the 1950s, when he was involved in bourgeois African nationalist affairs.' This is an altogether bizarre interpretation of the man and his work.

Guerin wrote asking her if it were true that George intended to stay in Africa, but she could only reply that 'our plans at the moment are fluid'.[66] By August, though, Padmore announced to Dobson that he was winding up his affairs and moving to Accra, despite the fact that he recently had started yet another enterprise, the Pan-African News Agency, and was fretting over the prospects for Eric Williams and West Indian federation. Tales told about Nkrumah in the British press were lies, he assured Dobson. 'The PM has taken firm action against certain aliens whom the police have discovered trying to stir-up tribalist divisions in the country and undermine the Government. They tried before independence when the British press gave widespread publicity to the danger of civil war. There was never any such danger and today the overwhelming majority of the people are 100 per cent behind the Government.'[67] He went on to persuade readers of the *Socialist Leader* to accept his assurances. Nkrumah, he wrote on September 26, was 'the George Washington, the Father of his country'. History would judge him favourably. The 'barrage of lies, distortions, innuendoes and downright vilification' which Fleet Street constructed was but part of the imperialist campaign to create unrest in the newest nation. *The Crisis* reprinted this essay in December for American readers.

Though Ghana came first, Padmore still retained an interest in Nigeria. He hoped that Dobson would be able to work out something with an American publisher, as he needed the money, especially since he had given up journalism in order to finish a cautionary book. The Nigerians 'are in such a tribal mess that I want to focus attention on the situation there before the next conference takes place. It is as little as I can do for Nigeria.'[68] A year earlier, he had told Guerin that he was worried about the Nigerian proclivity for pomp, which fitted in so nicely with British plans.

The Tories despatched the Queen to Nigeria to get a promise that even after independence they will remain in the Commonwealth. That is all they are concerned about—their sterling balances and trade. The colonials can have the rest—flag, national anthem and diplomatic representation abroad. The British are very pragmatic people. After all, it is the natives who pay for all those trappings of nationhood. It is the Nigerians who pay the £700,000 for the Royal circus. The British attitude is: if they (the natives) want a Royal jamboree, then let them pay. They [the British] are not the losers. And everybody is happy.[69]

The Nigerian book was never finished, though Padmore accepted an advance from Dobson and continued to mention it as an obligation to Azikiwe and the Nigerian people.'

In the autumn of 1957 it was public knowledge that he would become Nkrumah's adviser on African affairs. He cleared out his possessions in Cranleigh Street, in the process throwing out many personal papers and dispersing parts of his library (e.g. his annotated copy of Ormsby-Gore's 1926 West African report to parliament).[70] Dr David Pitt, a West Indian physician active in Parliamentary Labour Party affairs, whose surgery also sheltered nationalist groups, gave a small party in November, and the guests surprised Padmore with a briefcase. Only C. L. R. James represented the pre-war crowd. Most people there never saw Padmore again. His London period—that is, nearly all his adult life—was over. Soon he was in Accra, and the familiar stationery with the Cranleigh House stamp was replaced by notepaper from the Prime Minister's Office. Dorothy followed him out in the New Year. 'At long last I am able to drop you a few lines', he wrote to Dobson after Christmas. 'From the time of my arrival I have been very busy trying to organise my department and preparing the despatch of my first delegation to the Afro-Asian Peoples' Conference in Cairo. . . . The weather is very hot but the country is very quiet and making progress.'[71]

But Padmore was disturbed to find there was substantial Ghanaian opposition to his presence. He was West Indian, and there were too many of them prominent in Accra—economic advisers such as Arthur Lewis, press agents such as Sam Morris, and others who held senior posts in local administration and the judiciary. There is some indication that Nkrumah considered appointing Padmore to a cabinet post, but he was unable to persuade his colleagues to accept the notion and therefore turned to the idea of making Padmore a personal adviser in the Prime Minister's Office. While this saved face, it did not measurably increase Padmore's stature among Ghanaian civil servants, who, especially in the Foreign Ministry, resented the extra-bureaucratic influence he exerted over Nkrumah.

One of his first conflicts concerned salary. Padmore was disappointed to receive £1500, the maximum for his grade, but far below what he considered commensurate with his responsibilities. He had nothing, and was used to it, but he was convinced that a large salary was one means by which he could overawe his critics in the CPP. If he could not be a member of the regular civil service, then at least he could establish the importance of his extraordinary appointment. Nkrumah might listen to him, but others would do so only so long as he appeared independently powerful. Ultimately, the figure of £2100 was settled on, but the negotiations so disturbed him that, according to his nephew, Padmore was ready to quit Ghana and cast his lot with the Sudanese.[72] As Colin Legum, the *Observer*'s Commonwealth correspondent, recalls those early months: 'There was never a time when there was no pressure on G.P. to leave.'[73]

He set about establishing a small, flexible office composed of himself, his old friend Makonnen (yet another 'American') and James Markham, a young independent-minded Ghanaian. Markham was an Ewe who had read economics at London University, had been in jail for political action during 1948, and had been appointed editor of the CPP *Accra Evening News* in 1949. In 1951 he had helped Nkrumah's associate Gbedemah organise the election campaign which made the imprisoned Nkrumah first African Minister for Government Business in the Gold Coast. Markham had attended the Bandung Conference in 1955 and stayed in the east for two years. His wife was a Liberian of Negro American parentage.[74] These three men shared serious doubts about the socialist convictions of many CPP luminaries, nor were they altogether discreet in their criticisms. The ostentation and arrogance which early characterised many of these leaders was doubly distasteful to Padmore, who ridiculed their small-time pomp and objected to their definition of socialism. With this in mind, he did what he could to instill proper views in the CPP youth. The organ he concentrated upon was the National Association of Socialist Students' Organisation (NASSO), a body formed in Britain by Nkrumah and his associates. After Nkrumah's return to the Gold Coast this body remained the principal overseas study group dedicated to independence and a socialist revolution. Makonnen and Padmore did what they could to guide NASSO, and they derived comfort from Nkrumah's own unvarying attendance at weekly Wednesday-evening discussions.

The principal legacy which Padmore left this body was an unfinished manuscript on the origins of socialism and its application to the African scene.[75] It recapitulated much of what he had written since 1938 and may be regarded as his legacy to the country of his adoption. The village, he declared, must remain the basic unit. Large co-operative farming schemes, à la Gezira in Sudan, of course may be adopted, and even individual farmers may be tolerated, 'but whatever form is adopted, it is necessary that the village shall be the focal point of the surrounding farming community, and shall provide the social and cultural amenities which will bring town life to the countryside and thereby save the drift away from the land and the rural areas'. It would take a conscious effort to undo the colonial heritage, to eradicate the evils of capitalist greed, he wrote, but it could be done, provided the CPP remained a socialist vanguard party. Necessarily, Ghana would rely upon foreign capital and expertise for a period, but even so the leadership could 'make socialism a reality for the people of Ghana and an example to the rest of Africa'.

> Ghana is rich in capital which consists of her natural resources plus her labour power. Yet we cannot escape a period of austerity in order to harness this capital for constructing our socialist pattern of society. But how to attain this austerity? We must forgo those things which are not essential by imposing heavy taxation on luxury goods. Let those who want them pay for their ostentation.[76]

These views were not popular among Nkrumah's entourage, and Padmore's difficulties were increased when his distasteful puritanism was coupled with his rumoured Trotskyism. A late-comer to CPP office, Tawia Adamafio, and a rising trade unionist, John Tettegah, led the group which privately attacked the West Indian clique and gradually turned NASSO into a sort of Stalinist group. Their neutralism was decidedly of the eastern sort and Padmore's strictures on the two cold war blocs and warnings about Soviet intentions irritated these Ghanaian ideologues.

Padmore, then, rapidly found himself in conflict with a host of enemies in the party, the civil service, the cabinet and even NASSO. According to Legum, the Foreign Office refused to let Padmore use their cable service and denied him access to their files. No doubt, much of this was not sinister. After all, bureaucrats necessarily would have a horror of the unorthodox approach practised by this ex-Comintern figure. But it did not make Padmore's task any easier and, though he did not complain, his first letter to Dobson after arriving in Ghana was unusually terse.

Dobson next heard from him in March, by which time Padmore had flown to Liberia, North Africa and the Middle East. 'My books are in demand here', he gleefully wrote to his publisher from Khartoum.[77] On this trip he visited Israel, where he met his former Comintern colleague Berger, who shortly before had been released from a twenty-two year sojourn in various Soviet prison camps. Berger recalls that Padmore expressed private doubts about many of those surrounding Nkrumah, though his loyalty to the leader was undiminished.[78] Though he never wrote about his view of the Israeli question, certain things suggest that Padmore favoured the Jewish side of the dispute, or at least sought Israeli aid for Ghanaian development. Certainly Ghanaian–Israeli relations were best and Ghanaian–Egyptian relations worst during Padmore's stint at Flagstaff House. Several explanations spring to mind: Padmore worried about fascism and military rulers, he approved the socialist content of Israeli doctrine, he distrusted Nasser's flirtation with the communist camp and disliked Nasser's apparent desire to diminish Nkrumah's African role, he did not fear Israeli expansionism, and he admired the way overseas Jews supported the austere zionist state.[79] In any case, there is no doubt that Padmore was unpopular in Egypt and quite possibly may have planned to stay away from the second meeting of the All-African Peoples' Organisation (AAPO) which was scheduled to meet in Tunis early in 1960. He did what he could, and very effectively too, to hamper the Egyptians at the first meeting of the AAPO (Accra, December 1958) by reducing their proposed delegation's strength from a hundred to five.[80]

Padmore had flown about the continent during the first months of 1958 to prepare for the April meeting of independent African states. 'The arrangements . . . are largely in my hands', he told

Dobson, and, since many of the figures mentioned in *Pan-Africanism or Communism?* would attend the meeting in Accra, he asked his publisher to send additional copies of the book out to Ghana.[81] The meeting, which began on April 15, marked the first attempt to erect a bridge across the Sahara. Of the eight states which sent representatives, five were 'Arab'; only Ghana, Liberia and Ethiopia qualified as 'black' African polities, and the latter was merely beginning to accept this classification. Though Israel posed difficulties, differences were papered over, and the conferees adopted a series of resolutions, especially in support of the Algerian National Liberation Front and critical of South Africa.[82]

Padmore's books unfortunately did not arrive until the conference closed, but he was too busy to worry over lost sales. In June, he accompanied Nkrumah on his tour of seven African states,[83] and in the next month he attended a political rally in Dahomey.[84] In September, he wrote to Dobson again: 'We are in the throes of planning an All-African Peoples' Conference to be held here in Accra, and I would like to get from you to arrive here within the next month 500 copies of the colonial edition of *Britain —Africa's Third Empire* [*sic*, an interesting slip]. They should be posted to me, c/o the Prime Minister's Office, and should be sent in packages of 100 each, so that we don't have too much trouble with the Customs.'[85]

Dr Edwin Munger, who reported this conference for the American Universities' Field Staff,[86] says that Padmore indeed was the 'chief workhorse' there. An 'unusually well-informed African adviser', Padmore's presence in Ghana caused certain difficulties in the conduct of foreign policy. His own office handled African matters, while the Ministry of Foreign Affairs dealt with non-African arrangements. So long as Nkrumah held the Foreign Affairs portfolio himself, it did not matter that his closest confidant looked after African business. But when Nkrumah handed the Ministry to Kojo Botsio, as he had done recently, certain frictions naturally arose. Munger was impressed with Padmore's constant talk of communism versus nationalism. Discussing the desire of certain states to pack the conference with communists, Padmore allowed that he 'wasn't head of the Negro Section of the Comintern all those years not to know their tactics'. According to Munger,

Padmore was worried about the probable attendance of DuBois, whose communist message undoubtedly would be received with deference, such was the old man's prestige among young Africans. There is no reason to doubt the correctness of Professor Munger's report, but it does reveal a third stage in Padmore's relationship with DuBois. No doubt DuBois's decision to become a communist so late in life struck Padmore as a reversal of the natural order of political development, but it still is hard to reconcile with his earlier adulation of the 'father of Pan-Africanism'.

Another American who interviewed Padmore a month or so later gave an even more puzzling account of the Prime Minister's adviser. Late in February Smith Hempstone, then of the Institute for Current World Affairs and today with the African Bureau of the Chicago *Daily News*, had a very unsympathetic time with him. As he later recalled it:

I talked with him in his office, one of those typical wood-and-iron ramshackle Gold Coast buildings on stilts, just behind the new American Embassy. It was very hot and Padmore was in his shirtsleeves, revealing a set of bright red suspenders (he did not ask me to remove my coat and I sweltered through the conversation). As I mentioned in my newsletter, he looked 'tired and shriveled' (he died in less than a year). His accent and his mannerisms were those of an American Negro rather than a West Indian. He gave the impression of being arrogant and doctrinaire and was difficult to converse with, having a tendency to lecture rather than talk. He lacked the innate courtesy of the African, failing to offer the usual tea and a smoke, while he enjoyed both. He seemed sincere in his views, but rather out of touch with the new generation of African nationalists, with the exception of Nkrumah, of course, to whom he was very close. I have a feeling that Nkrumah's reliance on Padmore as an ideologue contributed to the Ghanaian leader's failure to gain real control of the Pan-Africanist movement. By this I mean that if Nkrumah himself had taken the trouble to ascertain the thinking of the other African leaders on the subject of Pan-Africanism, rather than relying on Padmore's interpretation of what the shape of Pan-Africanism should be, Nkrumah might have more stature than he has today.[87]

This version of Padmore is so badly in disagreement with every-one's accounts of his London days that one can only suppose either that the tropics did not agree with him or that Hempstone did not. Whether Padmore had seen the reports which formed the basis of Hempstone's later book (in London, *The New Africa*; in New York, *Africa, Angry Young Giant*) seems unlikely, but Hempstone's impatience with African failure and his penchant for Cold War interpretations may very well have been noticed by Padmore. The man who wrote: 'Pour me a double Manhattan and call me Senator McCarthy, but I get the impression from all this that the Pan-African movement, upon which so many hopes rest and which could be doing so much good, is being directed either by commu-nists or fools. Possibly both' might very well alienate lesser men than Padmore. It bears thinking about before one leaps to per-sonality change or the emergence of long-suppressed hubris for an explanation of Padmore's rudeness.

There is no doubt that he was courted by the representatives of all sorts of special interest. For the first time since his Kremlin days he had space, money and a staff, a satisfying end to his self-imposed task of African emancipation. If these things seemed fitting to those who knew Padmore's career and credentials, undoubtedly they appeared grossly inappropriate to others who resented the influence which this West Indian outsider disposed of.

In April and May 1959 Padmore attended Nkrumah on his state visit to newly independent Guinea. There, in Conakry, the steering committee of the All-African Peoples' Organisation began its first session on April 15.[88] A month later Padmore was able to announce that the next session would convene in Cairo in June. Ghana would be represented by the trade unionist, John Tettegah, and the Foreign Minister, Botsio. This, considering Padmore's special responsibility for African affairs, seemed odd, an exemplification of Munger's observation.[89] That something was wrong seems clear from the deportation of the British journalist Russell Warren Howe (today a correspondent for the *Washington Post*), supposedly for a story which he sold to the London *Sunday Times* in which he remarked that Padmore's role was resented by the AAPO represen-tatives.[90] Perhaps it was true that young Ghanaians deferred to Padmore, as one of his obituary commentators noted, but his worldly wisdom and enormous memory of books appealed most to those not competing with him for the Prime Minister's ear. Whatever else he was, Padmore clearly was not at all like Peter Abrahams's pathetic Tom Lanwood in *A Wreath for Udomo*.

That July Padmore went to the village of Saniquellie in Liberia for the meeting of the heads of state of Liberia, Guinea and Ghana. It was a miserable location and, though everyone came down with dysentery, Padmore, for some years never in good health and usually ill since moving to Accra, suffered most. He was, besides, discouraged at the increasingly apparent obstacles in the path of Pan-African unity, and the declaration of Saniquellie, which stressed the maintenance of national identity in any community of African states, did little to allay his misgivings. He never overcame his fears regarding Nigerian tribalism, and now he suspected that Ghana could not enforce the necessary amalgamation of African territories. He was sick, he was disappointed, he was uncomfortable in his public life and, according to some, unhappy in his private circumstances. By summer's end, he was too ill to procrastinate longer, and in September he asked Nkrumah to give him time to fly to London for a medical examination. When he arrived at Dr Clarke's New Barnet house, his distended belly was painfully obvious to the physician, who committed him to University College Hospital on Sunday, September 20.

There was severe liver deterioration. Padmore had a history of hepatitis. He took little or no alcohol and, according to Clarke, certainly showed no signs of poisoning. (This rumour circulated rapidly, and still does.) On the Wednesday evening, though he fought for life, Padmore was too tired and he slipped from a coma into death, rather more rapidly than Clarke had anticipated though he had never doubted the outcome.

The funeral service, with about two hundred in attendance, was held at the Golders Green Crematorium on Monday, September 28, and the ashes were flown to Ghana at the Prime Minister's request. There they were interred at Christiansborg Castle on October 4. In an emotional voice Nkrumah said 'when I first met George Padmore in London some fifteen years ago, we both realised from the very beginning that we thought along the same lines and talked the same language. There existed between us that rare affinity for which one searches for so long but seldom finds in another human being. We became friends at the moment of our meeting and our friendship developed into that indescribable relationship that exists between two brothers.'[91] Earlier, on the Ghana Radio service, Nkrumah had prophesied that 'one day the whole of Africa will surely be free and united and when the final tale is told the significance of George Padmore's work will be revealed'.[92] Nkrumah also announced that Padmore's office would be elevated into a Bureau of African Affairs with Kofi Baako as its first director. At David Astor's curiously British request, Clarke wrote up an obituary for *The Times*, and there Padmore lay, enshrined in one-third of a column of the paper most typical of all he had struggled against since his youth in the heat and clear skies of Trinidad.

It only remained for the Ghanaians to institutionalise him, which they quickly did.* Padmore, the appealing young man, the international revolutionary, the bookish activist, the elder of the anti-colonial family, had become in death the principal follower of Nkrumah, the most literate and persuasive of those who recognised and proclaimed Osagyefo's genius. The man himself was quickly forgotten; indeed, his entire pre-1957 career was shelved by friends and enemies alike, who wished to concentrate on the glamorous-seeming last years in Ghanaian employment. From my viewpoint, this was not the capstone of a career so much as the final stage of a preoccupation, merely one aspect of a rich and complicated personality's progress through the world. Padmore died the father of African emancipation, but he lived as far more: the expositor of the black man's dignity, the nagging conscience of a white man's world. Malcolm Nurse/George Padmore is a fit companion of Blyden and Sylvester Williams.

* See, for example, the *Evening News*, Accra, September 23, 1964, for the way in which Padmore has come to play the role of John the Baptist.

Notes and References

(Full publication details are listed in the Bibliography)

I: FROM TRINIDAD TO NEW YORK: NURSE BECOMES PADMORE

1. See the College history, *Centenary Record of the Holy Ghost Fathers in Trinidad and of St Mary's College, 1863–1963*, Port of Spain 1963.
2. Copy given to author by assistant registrar of Fisk University.
3. Documents in author's possession.
4. For Blyden, see Lynch, Hollis, "Edward W. Blyden: Pioneer West African Nationalist", *Journal of African History*, Vol. VI, No. 3, 1965.
5. Letter, John Dillingham to W. C. Craver, copy in possession of Padmore's daughter, Mrs Blyden Cowart.
6. Letter, assistant registrar of Fisk University to author, December 18, 1965.
7. *The Crisis*, April 1925.
8. Jones-Quartey, K. A. B., *A Life of Azikiwe*, p. 96. Writer identified by internal evidence.
9. For Garvey's American period, see Cronon, Edmund, *Black Moses*.
10. See Padmore's review of Scott Nearing's *Black America* in *Labor Unity*, March 8, 1929.
11. See Pope, Liston, *Millhands and Preachers: A Study of Gastonia*.
12. Quoted in *Pan-Africanism or Communism?*, p. 319.
13. *Report of the Fourth Congress of the Red International of Labour Unions*, July 1928.
14. Red International of Labour Unions, *Resolutions and Decisions, 1923* (Second Congress), London 1923.
15. For photos and extensive coverage of this meeting, see Italiaander, Rolf, *Schwarze Haut im Roten Griff*, and also, of course, Brockway, Fenner, *Inside the Left*.
16. (New York) *State Training School document* in CP collection in Michigan State University Library.
17. See Kimble, David, *A Political History of Ghana*, p. 549, and Nolan, William, *Communism versus the Negro*, p. 46.

18. For a good résumé of the proceedings—which do not mention Padmore—see "A l'Assaut des Colonies", Bulletin 6, Antwerp, November 15, 1929, of the militantly anti-communist Société d'Etudes Politiques, Economiques et Sociales. This also contains some valuable background on LAI meetings.

19. See *Daily Worker* (NY), August 24, 1929, for Padmore's cautionary essay on the American Federation of Labor's expulsion of 'nigger-lovers'.

20. *Afro-American*, October 15, 1938.

21. See Padmore's article, "Some shortcomings in our TU work among Negroes in the US."

22. *New Leader*, August 29, 1942, obituary on the Cuban trade unionist Julio Sandalio Junco, 'my colleague for many years'.

23. See Homer Smith's opaque and disappointing *Black Man in Red Russia*. Information from interview, Smith and Charles Thornton (author's student), August 7, 1965.

24. *New Leader*, October 3, 1942.

2: TOP NEGRO DESCENDING: PADMORE BECOMES AN UNPERSON

1. See *Daily Worker* (NY), August 7, 1930; *Pan-Pacific Monthly*, No. 38, September–October 1930; *First International Trade Union Committee of Negro Workers: Resolutions*.

2. Brockway, op. cit., p. 261.

3. Valtin, Jan, *Out of the Night*, pp. 275–6.

4. *Negro Worker*, July 1931.

5. Memoir, Y. Berger to author, March 7, 1967.

6. Ibid.

7. Ibid.

8. *Negro Worker*, October–November 1931; *The Communist*, February 1931, pp. 133–46.

9. Padmore, "American Imperialism Enslaves Liberia".

10. *New Leader*, September 13, 1941.

11. See Nyasa GOB/G85, February 19, 1932, and NR Sec/Nos. 1 and 3, May 1934.

12. *Encounter*, December 1959.

13. See *MIZAN Newsletter*, October 1964.

14. *The Communist*, June 1931.

15. Nyasa GOB/G85, June 30, 1931.

16. *International Press Correspondence* (*INPRECORR*), June 11, 1931.

17. Conference reported in *Negro Worker*, October–November 1931.

18. James, *Black Jacobins*, p. 7; *INPRECORR*, July 23, 1931.

19. *Negro Worker*, June 1932.

20. Cunard, Nancy, *Negro Anthology*, p. 260.

21. Interview, C. A. Smith and author, September 18, 1964.

22. Letter, Nancy Cunard to author, November 1964.

23. Ibid.

24. *Daily Telegraph*, March 18, 1965.

25. Cunard, *Negro Anthology*, p. 144.

Notes and References

26. Ibid., p. 146.
27. Ibid., p. 147.
28. Ibid., pp. 239–41.
29. See the obituary by "Genet" (Janet Flanner) in the *New Yorker*, April 3, 1965, and various tributes in the *Afro-American* issues of March 1934.
30. *New Leader*, January 9, 1946; substantially the same version may be found in *Controversy*, July 1937.
31. The same story was recalled by C. A. Smith in an interview with the author, September 18, 1964.
32. Letter, Padmore to Daniel Guerin, April 4, 1956.
33. *Negro Worker*, June 1934.
34. Letter, Padmore to DuBois, February 17, 1934.
35. Information supplied by the Liberian Padmore's son (author's student) and wife. See also Legum, Colin, *Bandung, Cairo and Accra*, p. 10.
36. Letter, Nancy Cunard to author, November 1964.
37. Browder in *The Crisis*, December 1935.
38. Note by Nancy Cunard, "Books and People", sent to author in February 1965, shortly before her death.
39. Ford, J. W., "Is Japan the Champion of the Colored Races?".
40. Padmore, *Pan-Africanism or Communism?*, p. 324.

3: THE HARD YEARS: BLACK BROTHERS IN LONDON

1. Letter, Padmore to DuBois, February 17, 1934.
2. *WASU*, November 1935.
3. Letter, Aptheker to author, January 20, 1965.
4. *Negro Worker*, August and September 1934; David Vaughan, *Black Victory*, London 1950; *The Crisis*, June 1940; *New Leader*, June 14, 1941; League of Coloured Peoples *Annual Report* for 1938.
5. See Julian's book, *Black Eagle*, Jarrolds, London 1964.
6. "War in Africa", August 1935—an interview which William Jones of the *Afro-American*, Benjamin Careathers and Ford, representing the League of Struggle for Negro Rights, had with Tecle Hawariate, Ethiopian delegate to the League of Nations.
7. Letter, Subasinghe to author, August 17, 1964.
8. See Reynolds, Reginald, *My Life and Crimes*; Brockway, op. cit.; interview, author and Goldwater, May 22, 1964; interview, author and Ridley, September 1964.
9. Nyasa s2/3/34, June 1935.
10. Nyasa Archives, s2/15/35.
11. Letter, R. Bridgeman to author, September 22, 1964.
12. Nyasa s2/1/38, 27/1/38.
13. "Give Away the Colonies! Cranks—and a Few Others—in Conference", *East Africa*, November 7, 1935.
14. From Langton collection in Michigan State University Library; letter dated June 5, 1935.
15. Interviews, Padley and Ridley and author, September 1964.

16. See, for example, *New Leader*, May 20, 1938.
17. Letter, Bridgeman to author, September 22, 1964.
18. Letter, Subasinghe to author, August 17, 1964.
19. Interview, Kumria and author, September 1964.
20. See Brockway, op. cit., pp. 325–7; also Reginald Reynolds's review, *New Leader*, July 2, 1937.
21. Letter, Padmore to Guerin, August 9, 1955.
22. Letter, Lewis to author, August 19, 1965.
23. *Afro-American*, February 4, 1939.
24. From inside cover of Padmore's "Hands off the Protectorates".
25. Nyasa s2/1/38.
26. Interview, Smith and author, September 18, 1964.
27. Coleman, James, *Nigeria: Background to Nationalism*, p. 208.
28. NCCL *Annual Report*, 1938.
29. *Law Reports: Appeals Cases, 1940; House of Lords, Judicial Committee of the Privy Council*, pp. 231–41; also in 56 *TLR* 215.
30. See *Negro Worker*; Akyeampong, *Liberty*; Padmore, *Gold Coast Revolution*; Rogers, Joel A., *World's Great Men of Color*, Vol. 1, pp. 270–4.
31. *New Leader*, February 25, 1938.
32. Memoir, McNair to author, May 1964.
33. *Controversy*, March 1938.
34. *Controversy*, February and March 1938.
35. *New Leader*, April 24, 1938.
36. *Defender*, July 16, 1938.
37. *Defender*, July 23, 1938.
38. *New Leader*, September 30, 1938; photo of Padmore in *Defender*, October 15, 1938.
39. *New Leader*, September 23, 1938.
40. *Defender*, October 1, 1938; interview, Lochard and Thornton, August 7, 1965.
41. Letter, Cunard to author, February 14, 1965.
42. *Defender*, November 12, 1938.
43. *Controversy*, May and June 1938.
44. *New Leader*, January 20, 1939; letter, Guerin to author, February 22, 1965.
45. Nyasa s2/1/38, April 1939.
46. *New Leader*, June 2, 1939.
47. Interview, Dorothy Abrahams and author, September 1964.
48. Memoir, McNair to author, May 1964.
49. Ibid.
50. Cited in Nyasa s2/3/34.
51. *New Leader*, October 21 and 31, and November 24, 1939.

4: 'THE WORST RACKET INVENTED BY MAN'

1. *New Leader*, December 15, 1939.
2. *New Leader*, March 8, 1940.

Notes and References

3. Memoir, McNair to author, May 1964.
4. *New Leader*, January 25, 1941.
5. LCP *Newsletter*, No. 23, August 1941, replacing the original *The Keys* (1933–39) which, in 1935 and 1936, had been edited by the budding economist Arthur Lewis, then studying at the LSE.
6. Memoir, McNair to author, May 1964.
7. *New Leader*, May 30, 1940.
8. *Anti-Slavery Reporter*, April 1941.
9. LCP *Newsletter*, No. 9.
10. See *New Leader*, October 3, 1940.
11. *New Leader*, September 19 and December 28, 1940, and January 4 and May 3, 1941.
12. *New Leader*, March 29, 1941.
13. Letter, Cunard to author, October 15, 1964.
14. Ibid.
15. *New Leader*, February 15, 1941.
16. *New Leader*, March 8 and 15, 1941; also *Anti-Slavery Reporter*, October 1941.
17. *New Leader*, July 26, 1941.
18. *New Leader*, September 6, 1941.
19. Information from interviews, Dr Clarke and author and Dorothy Abrahams and author, September 1964.
20. Programme in *New Leader*, July 26, 1941.
21. *New Leader*, December 27, 1941.
22. *New Leader*, January 24, 1942.
23. *Tribune*, February 27, 1942.
24. *New Leader*, January 3, 1942.
25. *Tribune*, May 15, 1942.
26. *WASU*, May 1943, report of meeting July 29–30, 1942.
27. *New Leader*, October 17, 1940.
28. Letter, Cunard to author, February 14, 1965.
29. *The Crisis*, March 1941.
30. Padmore, *White Man's Duty*, p. 48.
31. *New Leader*, March 6, 13 and 20, 1943.
32. *Tribune*, October 1, 1943.
33. See Hooker, "The Role of the Labour Department in the Birth of Trade Unionism in Northern Rhodesia", *International Review of Social History*, Vol. 10, Pt. 1, 1965.
34. *New Leader*, November 15 and 22, 1941.
35. *New Leader*, December 4, 1943.
36. *New Leader*, October 23, 1943, and *WASU*, June 1944.
37. *Anti-Slavery Reporter*, October 1943.

5: ANTI-STALINIST DEFENDS THE SOVIET UNION

1. *New Leader*, July 25, 1940.
2. *New Leader*, May 9, 1942.
3. Letter, Subasinghe to author, August 17, 1964.

4. Padmore, *Pan-Africanism or Communism?*, p. 300.
5. *Tribune*, April 23, 1943.
6. *The Crisis*, November 1942.
7. *The Crisis*, June 1943.
8. For the same points, see also his review in *Tribune*, September 1, 1944, of Alexander Campbell's *Empire in Africa*.
9. Memoir, McNair to author, May 1964.
10. *Left*, February 1940.
11. Letter, Tertius Chandler to author, September 16, 1964.
12. Letter, Padmore to Dobson, June 28, 1944.
13. Letter, Padmore to Dobson, April 22, 1944.
14. Letter, Padmore to Dobson, June 28, 1944.
15. Letter, Padmore to Dobson, June 28 and July 27, 1944.
16. Letter, Subasinghe to author, August 17, 1964.
17. Letter, Ethel Mannin to author, September 9, 1964.
18. *Socialist Leader*, August 26, 1950.
19. Letter, Padmore to Dobson, January 23, 1946.
20. Interview, Padley and author, September 4, 1964.
21. Akyeampong, H. K., *Liberty, A Page from the Life of J.B.*, p. 16.
22. Letter, Padmore to Dobson, January 19, 1945.
23. Letter, Padmore to Dobson, August 16, 1944.

6: THE ROAD TO MANCHESTER

1. *Left*, June 1943, and *New Leader*, December 12, 1944.
2. Quoted in LCP *Newsletter*, May 1944.
3. Letter, Padmore to Dobson, August 16, 1944.
4. For James's subsequent deportation, see his study of Hermann Melville, *Mariners, Renegades and Castaways*, chapter 7.
5. *Defender*, August 29, 1942.
6. *Courier*, November 25, 1944.
7. Letter, Padmore to Dobson, October 26, 1944.
8. Letter, Padmore to Dobson, March 29, 1944; letter, Dobson to Padmore, March 31, 1944.
9. Letter, Padmore to Dobson, October 10, 1944.
10. Letter, Padmore to DuBois, August 21, 1950; letter, DuBois to Padmore, September 18, 1950; interview, Dobson and author, September 7, 1964.
11. *Defender*, March 31, 1945; *New Leader*, March 31, 1945.
12. See Thyra Edwards, "The ILO and Post-War Planning for the African Colonies", *The Crisis*, July 1944.
13. Douglas Rogers in *New Leader*, February 24, 1945.
14. For the proceedings, see Padmore, ed., *Voice of Coloured Labour*, introduction by Padmore dated July 20. See also *The Crisis*, April 1945, and *West Africa*, March 31, 1945.
15. Padmore in *Courier*, February 24, 1945.
16. Padmore in *Courier*, March 3, 1945.
17. *Defender*, March 17, 1945.

Notes and References

18. Letter, Subasinghe to author, August 17, 1964.
19. Printed in revised edition of *White Man's Duty*.
20. Padmore, ed., *Colonial and Coloured Unity*, p. 11.
21. Quoted in Padmore, *Pan-Africanism or Communism?*, p. 157.
22. See his graceful tribute in *Pan-Africanism or Communism?*, p. 365.
23. Proceedings printed in the second edition of *White Man's Duty*; the manifesto appears in part in *Left*, June 1945.
24. From a photocopy supplied by Mrs Dorothy Abrahams, librarian for *The Economist*.
25. *Defender*, May 26, 1945.
26. See Padmore, ed., *Colonial and Coloured Unity*; *Anti-Slavery Reporter*, October 1945; Jones-Quartey, op. cit.; Coleman, op. cit.
27. *New Leader*, July 21, 1945; *WASU*, March 1946.
28. Letter to editor of *Socialist Leader*, February 28, 1948.
29. Interview, Mrs Klopper and author, September 11, 1964.
30. Phillips, John, *Kwame Nkrumah and the Future of Africa*, p. 82.
31. Nkrumah, *Ghana, the Autobiography of Kwame Nkrumah*, p. 53.
32. Interview, Dr Malcolm Luke and author, September 1964.
33. *Defender*, September 1, 1945.
34. Padmore, ed., *Colonial and Coloured Unity*, p. 25.
35. *Defender*, September 29, 1945.
36. *New Leader*, October 13, 1945.
37. Nkrumah, *Autobiography*, p. 54.
38. Padmore, ed., *Colonial and Coloured Unity*, pp. 6 and 7.
39. *New Leader*, November 3, 1945.
40. *Defender*, December 1, 1945.
41. DuBois, W. E. B., *Dusk of Dawn*, p. 303.
42. *Defender*, December 1, 1945.

7: GOLD COAST ASCENDANT

1. Nkrumah, *Autobiography*, p. 57, and *Africa Must Unite*, p. 135.
2. *WASU Magazine*, Summer 1947.
3. *Socialist Leader*, September 21, 1946.
4. Nkrumah, *Autobiography*, pp. 62–3.
5. Nkrumah, *Towards Colonial Freedom*, Foreword.
6. Crocker, W. R., *Self-Government for the Colonies*, London 1949, pp. 87–8.
7. Letter, Dorothy Pizer to Guerin, July 22, 1946.
8. Letter, Padmore to Dobson, August 18, 1946.
9. Letter, Padmore to Guerin, October 29, 1946; interview, Luke and author, September 1964.
10. *Defender*, September 28, 1946, with autographed photo of Ho.
11. Letter, Cunard to author, February 14, 1965.
12. *Politics*, April–May 1946.
13. Letter, Padmore to Guerin, November 8, 1946.
14. *Socialist Leader*, September 28 and October 5, 1946.

15. *The Crisis*, October 1946; see also Padmore's essay "Trusteeship—The New Imperialism".
16. *Pan-Africa*, No. 1, January 1947.
17. *New Leader*, March 2, 1946.
18. Although easier to trace than his pre-war venture, *International African Opinion*, the British Museum holds only a broken file—1946–7: Nos. 3–5, 7 and 8; 1947–8: Nos. 3–14; 1948: Nos. 1–6.
19. *Defender*, February 16, 1946.
20. LCP *Newsletter*, July 1946.
21. *Socialist Leader*, November 23, 1946; letter, Osman to author, July 3, 1964; see also Padmore's essay "Sudanese Want Independence", *The Crisis*, June 1947—a strong attack on Labour duplicity—and Osman's article in *Pan-Africa*, No. 2.
22. LCP *Newsletter*, January 1947.
23. Letter, Padmore to Dobson, March 5, 1947.
24. Ako Adjei in LCP *Newsletter*, August 1947; letter, James Gordon (of Dobson's firm) to NCCL, August 12, 1947.
25. See *Colonial Parliamentary Bulletin*, September/October/November 1947; *Socialist Leader*, September 20, 1947.
26. *Socialist Leader*, May 24, 1947.
27. Letter, Hale to author, September 28, 1964.
28. LCP *Newsletter*, June 1947.
29. Padmore, *Pan-Africanism or Communism?*, pp. 174–5; "Pan-Africanism and Ghana" in *United Asia, Magazine of Asian Affairs*, Bombay 1957, pp. 50–4.
30. LCP *Newsletter*, October 1947.
31. Letter, Brockway to author, February 17, 1964.
32. *Socialist Leader*, March 20, 1948.
33. *The Crisis*, July 1948.
34. Letter (on *African Press Agency* notepaper), Padmore to DuBois, February 23, 1948; now in DuBois papers.
35. *Socialist Leader*, June 26, 1948.

8: GHANA: THE MONTHS OF POWER

1. Quoted in prospectus for Padmore's *Africa: Britain's Third Empire*, which Dobson listed for publication in summer, 1949.
2. Letter, Padmore to Dobson, October 22, 1948; letter, Dobson to Nkrumah, February 24, 1949.
3. Letter, E. G. Sarsfield-Hall to Dobson, April 8, 1949.
4. Letter, Dobson to Sarsfield-Hall, April 11, 1949.
5. Letter (on *Colonial Parliamentary Bulletin* notepaper), Padmore to Dobson, undated.
6. Letter, Padmore to Dobson, December 22, 1948.
7. Letter, Padmore to Dobson, August 21, 1949; written from Makonnen's "Rendezvous Restaurant".
8. Letter, Padmore to Gordon, August 24, 1949.
9. Letter, Padmore to DuBois, October 31, 1949.

Notes and References

10. *Socialist Leader*, March 18, 1950.
11. Letter to Dobson, May 23, 1950.
12. Letter, Azikiwe to Dobson, April 27, 1950.
13. Letter, Padmore to DuBois, August 21, 1950; letter, DuBois to Padmore, September 18, 1950.
14. Letters, Padmore to DuBois and to Miss Alice Citron, secretary of the DuBois Defense Committee, January 8 and October 11, 1951.
15. Letter, Brockway to Griffiths, Colonial Secretary, November 29, 1950.
16. *The Crisis*, December 1948.
17. *Socialist Leader*, October 22, 1949, and March 13, 1954.
18. Letter, Padmore to DuBois, October 31, 1949.
19. Programme for ILP Summer School in author's possession.
20. *Socialist Leader*, June 30, 1951.
21. *Socialist Leader*, July 28, 1951.
22. Letter, Padmore to DuBois, January 8, 1951; see also St Clair Drake, "Rise of the Pan-African Movement", *Africa Special Report*, April 1958.
23. *Socialist Leader*, September 1, 1951.
24. *Socialist Leader*, September 1 and 29, 1951.
25. Letter, Padmore to Dobson, April 10, 1952.
26. Letter, Padmore to Dobson, Saturday the 7th (month unknown), 1953.
27. Letter, Dobson to Padmore, March 6, 1953.
28. Letter, Padmore to Dobson, July 23, 1954.
29. Letter, Creech Jones to author, July 26, 1964.
30. *WASU News Service*, 11, September 2, 1953. This publication began in August 1952 as a successor to *WASU*. It appeared sporadically: consecutively till February 1954, then again in May 1955, and seems to have expired (at least the British Museum series ends) in 1957. In 1953 it received some support from the International Union of Students.
31. For the campaign, see Austin, Dennis, *Politics in Ghana*, p. 200.
32. Letter, Padmore to DuBois, January 8, 1951; see also *Socialist Leader*, September 5 and 26, October 31 and December 19, 1953.
33. See Koinange, Mbiyu, *The People of Kenya Speak for Themselves*, Kenya Publication Fund, Detroit 1955.
34. Letter, Padmore to Guerin, November 23, 1953.
35. Letter, Padmore to DuBois, December 12, 1953; for a book which reflects the atmosphere during the Kabaka crisis, see Legum, Colin, *Must We Lose Africa?*.
36. Despatch from an unnamed special correspondent of the *Socialist Leader*, December 19, 1953.
37. *The Times*, December 30, 1953, and January 3, 1954.
38. For the background, see Austin, op. cit., pp. 164–6. The entire sequence is printed in *Socialist Leader*, January 30, 1954.
39. Letter, Padmore to Dobson, May 10, 1954.
40. Letter, Padmore to DuBois, March 10, 1955.

41. Letters, Padmore to Guerin, June 22 and 26, 1954.
42. Letter, Padmore to DuBois, December 3, 1954.
43. Letter, Padmore to Guerin, November 30, 1954.
44. Letter, Chandler to author, October 12, 1964.
45. Letter, Padmore to Guerin, December 30, 1954.
46. Letter, Padmore to Gordon, August 11, 1955.
47. Letter, Padmore to Dobson, December 15, 1955.
48. Letter, Padmore to Guerin, June 10, 1956.
49. Letter, Padmore to Guerin, January 21, 1957.
50. Letter, Dorothy Pizer to Guerin, July 16, 1956.
51. Austin, op. cit., pp. 316–62.
52. Letter, Padmore to Guerin, March 23, 1956.
53. Letter, Padmore to Guerin, April 20, 1956.
54. Letter, Padmore to Mrs Dobson, March 23, 1956.
55. Padmore, *Pan-Africanism or Communism?*, p. 338; letter, Padmore to Guerin, April 20, 1956.
56. Letter, Padmore to Guerin, June 10, 1956; *Socialist Leader*, June 23, 1956.
57. Letter, Padmore to Dobson, November 22, 1956.
58. Letter, Padmore to Guerin, April 20, 1956.
59. Interview, Dobson and author, September 7, 1964.
60. Review list given to author by Dobson.
61. Letter, Guerin to Padmore, September 18, 1956.
62. Letter, Padmore to Guerin, September 26, 1956.
63. Letter, Bunche to author, January 7, 1965.
64. Article in *Socialist Leader*, December 8, 1956; post-mortem in issue of May 10, 1957.
65. Letter, Padmore to Dobson, *c.* late March, 1957.
66. Letter, Pizer to Guerin, June 3, 1957.
67. Letter, Padmore to Dobson, August 26, 1957.
68. Letter, Padmore to Dobson, September 12, 1957.
69. Letter, Padmore to Guerin, February 21, 1956.
70. Given to author by Charles Lahr, Padmore's friend and ILP comrade.
71. Letter, Padmore to Dobson, December 29, 1957.
72. Interview, Luke and author, September 1964.
73. Letter, Legum to author, August 1966.
74. See Edwin Munger, "Jimmy Markham", and "The All-African Peoples' Conference". *Pace* Professor Munger, Markham never worked for the *Observer*, though he was put in touch with this paper by Colonial Office officials who recognised his abilities. (Letter, Legum to author, August 1966.)
75. See Friedland, William, and Rosberg, Carl, eds., *African Socialism*, Stanford University Press, Stanford 1964, appendix 1; also the essay in this volume by Legum, Colin, "Socialism in Ghana: a Political Interpretation", pp. 131–59.
76. Friedland and Rosberg, op. cit., p. 234.
77. Letter, Padmore to Dobson, March 13, 1958.

Notes and References

78. Letter, Berger to author, February 17, 1965; interview, Berger and author, June 6, 1966.
79. My impressions have been gained from a number of sources, particularly Padmore's letters to DuBois, Dobson and Guerin, but I wish to thank both Colin Legum and an American postgraduate student, Scott Thompson, for their own observations along these lines. It may also be revelant to note that Dorothy was Jewish.
80. Munger, "The All-African Peoples' Conference", op. cit.
81. Letter, Padmore to Dobson, March 22, 1958.
82. For the conference see Legum, Colin, *Pan-Africanism, A Short Political Guide*, pp. 41–2.
83. Letter, Padmore to Dobson, May 28, 1958.
84. Postcard, Padmore to Guerin from Cotonou, July 1958.
85. Letter, Padmore to Dobson, September 29, 1958.
86. Munger, "The All-African Peoples' Conference", op. cit.
87. Letter, Hempstone to author, April 19, 1964. His report is found in the confidential newsletter of the Institute for Current World Affairs, New York, SH–144, March 2, 1959. These reports are the basis of Hempstone's book.
88. *West Africa*, April 25, 1959.
89. *West Africa*, May 16, 1959.
90. *West Africa*, June 6, 1959.
91. Quoted in Arthur, John, *Freedom for Africa*, p. 61.
92. Quoted in Adamafio, Tawia, *Hands Off Africa!*, pp. 45–7.

Newspapers, Journals and Magazines Cited in Text

Africa and the World, London
Africa Special Report (from October 1960, *Africa Report*), Washington, DC
African Interpreter, Philadelphia
African Morning Post, Accra
African Sentinel, London
Afro-American, Baltimore (in 1938–39, Washington)
American Universities Field Staff Reports, New York
Anti-Imperialist Review, London and Brussels
Anti-Slavery Reporter, London
Colonial Parliamentary Bulletin: A Monthly Record of the Colonies in Westminster, London
Controversy (from 1939, *Left*), London
Coterie Clarion, Port of Spain, Trinidad
Courier, Pittsburgh
Daily News, Moscow
Daily Telegraph, London
Daily Worker, New York
Defender, Chicago
East Africa and Rhodesia, London
Encounter, London
Evening News, Accra
Fact, London
Gold Coast Leader, Accra
Herald, Fisk University, Nashville, Tennessee
Hilltop, Howard University, Washington, DC
Index, variously at Los Angeles, Hull and Georgetown, Guyana
International African Opinion, London
International Negro Workers' Review: see *Negro Worker*
International Press Correspondence (*INPRECORR*), London

Newspapers, Journals and Magazines Cited in Text

Journal of African History, London
La Race Nègre, Paris
LCP *Newsletter*: see *The Keys*
Left: see *Controversy*
Liberator: see *Negro Champion*
Negro Champion (from late 1929, *Liberator*), New York
Negro Worker (first two issues *International Negro Workers' Review*), Hamburg and at various times from 1933 to 1937 Copenhagen, Brussels, New York and Paris
New African, London
New Leader (from June 1946 *Socialist Leader*), London
New Statesman, London
New York Times, New York
New Yorker, New York
Pan-Africa, Manchester
Pan-Pacific Monthly, San Francisco
Politics, New York
Red International of Labour Unions, London
Socialist Leader: see *New Leader*
The Communist, London
The Crisis, New York
The Keys (from October 1939, LCP *Newsletter*), London
The Times, London
Tribune, London
United Asia, Magazine of Asian Affairs, Bombay
WASU (became *WASU News Service*, August 1952), London
Weekly Guardian, Port of Spain, Trinidad
West Africa, London
World, Atlanta

Bibliography

Books and Extended Pamphlets by Padmore

Africa: Britain's Third Empire, Dennis Dobson, London 1949

Africa and World Peace, Secker and Warburg, London 1937

ed., *Colonial and Coloured Unity, a Programme of Action: History of the Pan-African Congress*, Panaf Services, Manchester 1947; reprinted by Hammersmith Bookshop, London 1963

Gold Coast Revolution, Dennis Dobson, London 1953

How Britain Rules Africa, Wishart Books, London 1936

How Russia Transformed Her Colonial Empire, Dennis Dobson, London 1946

Life and Struggles of Negro Toilers, Red International of Labour Unions, London 1931

Pan-Africanism or Communism?, Dennis Dobson, London 1956

ed., *Voice of Coloured Labour*, Panaf Services, Manchester 1945

with Nancy Cunard, *White Man's Duty*, W. H. Allen, London 1942; enlarged and re-issued by Panaf Services, Manchester 1945

Journals Padmore Helped Found and/or Edit

Colonial Parliamentary Bulletin, private newsletter, London; founder and editor, 1946–48

Left (formerly *Controversy*), an organ of the Independent Labour Party group, London; co-editor (with Jon Evans) 1942–43

Negro Worker, Red International of Labour Unions for the International Trade Union Committee of Negro Workers, Hamburg; editor, volumes one and two, 1931–33

Most Important Articles by Padmore

"American Imperialism Enslaves Liberia", *The Communist*, February 1931

"An Introduction to South Africa", *Pan-Africa*, Vol. 11, Nos. 3–4, March–April 1948

Bibliography

"An Open Letter to Earl Browder", *The Crisis*, October 1935

"Bloodless Revolution on the Gold Coast", *The Crisis*, March 1952

"Blueprint of Post-War Anglo-American Imperialism", *Left*, October 1943

"British Labour and the Colonies", *The Crisis*, October 1945

"Colonial Policy that Saved Russia", *Tribune*, April 23, 1943

"Colonials Demand Britain's War Aims", *New Leader*, February 15, 1941

"Continuing Crisis in British Guiana", *Socialist Leader*, October 31, 1953

"Crisis in Buganda", *Socialist Leader*, December 19, 1953

"Ethiopia and World Politics", *The Crisis*, May 1935

"Facts Behind the Gold Coast Riots", *The Crisis*, July 1948

"Fascism in the Colonies", *Controversy*, February 1938

"Gastonia: its Significance for Negro Labor", *Daily Worker*, October 4, 1929

"Hands Off Liberia!", *Negro Worker*, October–November 1931

"Hands Off the Colonies!", *New Leader*, February 25, 1938

"Hands Off the Protectorates!", International Africa Service Bureau, London, *c.* July–August 1938

"Hands Off the Soviet Union!", *Left*, No. 41, April 1940

"Interview with Ho Chi Minh", *Defender*, September 28, 1946 (substantively republished as "The Story of Viet Nam", *Politics*, December 1946)

"Interview with the Umma Leaders", *Socialist Leader*, November 23, 1946

"Jamaica Rejects Sham 'Democratic' Constitution", *New Leader*, September 6, 1941

"Labour Imperialism and East Africa", *Labour Monthly*, Vol. XIII, Nos. 5 and 6, May and June 1931

"Madagascar Fights for Freedom", *Left*, No. 132, October 1947 (reprinted in *The Crisis*, December 1948)

Negro Workers and the Imperialist War—Intervention in the Soviet Union, Red International of Labour Unions, Hamburg 1931

"New Pattern of Imperialism", *New Leader*, December 4 and 11, 1943

"No Atlantic Charter for the Colonies", *New Leader*, January 24, 1942

"Not Nazism! Not Imperialism! But Socialism!", *New Leader*, December 27, 1941

"Oliver Stanley's Colonial Circus", *The Crisis*, October 10, 1943

"Pan-Africanism and Ghana", *United Asia, Magazine of Asian Affairs*, Special African edition, 1957

"Race Relations: Soviet and British", *The Crisis*, November 1942

Responses to a poll on "Vital Issues of the War", *Left*, No. 62, November 1941

Review of Scott Nearing's *Black America*, Vanguard, New York 1929, in *Labour Unity*, Communist Party, New York, August 3, 1929

"Review of the Peace Conference", *Pan-Africa*, No. 1, January 1947

"Russia Destroyed Her Empire!", *Tribune*, February 12, 1943

"Socialist Attitude to the Invasion of the USSR", *Left*, No. 60, September 1941

Black Revolutionary

"Some Shortcomings in Our T[rade] U[nion] Work Among Negroes in the US", *Red International of Labour Unions*, II, 2–3, May–June 1930

"The British Empire is the Worst Racket Yet Invented By Man", *New Leader*, December 15, 1939

"The Economics of Riots in South Africa", *Socialist Leader*, February 26, 1949

"The Missionary Racket in Africa", *The Crisis*, July 1935

"The Press Campaign Against Ghana", *Socialist Leader*, September 28, 1957 (reprinted in *The Crisis*, December 1957)

"The Trade Union Unity Convention and the Negro Masses", *Daily Worker*, August 27, 1929

"Trusteeship: the New Imperialism", *The Crisis*, October 1946

"Uncle Sam's Black Ward", *Tribune*, October 23, 1942

"We Gave Them Copper—They Gave Us Lead", *New Leader*, April 18, 1940

What is the International Trade Union Committee of Negro Workers?, Hamburg, n.d., prob. late 1931

"Whither the West Indies?", *New Leader*, March 29, 1941

"Why I Left", *Socialist Leader*, November 9, 1946

"Why I Oppose Conscription", *New Leader*, June 2, 1939

"Why Moors Help Franco", *New Leader*, May 20, 1938

"Why the RAF Has Dropped the Colour Bar", *New Leader*, January 25, 1941

GENERAL BIBLIOGRAPHY

(Minus items mentioned en passant)

"A Betrayer of the Negro Liberation Struggle", *Negro Worker*, June 1934

"A l'Assaut des Colonies—Le Communisme et le Congo Belge", *Bulletin de la Société d'Etudes Politiques, Economiques et Sociales*, Brussels, Vol. v, No. 6, November 1929

Abrahams, Peter, *A Wreath for Udomo*, Faber, London 1956

Adamafio, Tawia, *Hands Off Africa!*, Ministry of Local Government, Accra 1960

Akyeampong, H. K., *Liberty, A Page from the Life of J.B.*, privately printed, Accra 1960

Anon. (Dr C. Belfield Clarke), Padmore obituary, *The Times*, September 25, 1959

Arthur, John, *Freedom for Africa*, privately printed, Accra 1961

Austin, Dennis, *Politics in Ghana, 1946–1960*, Oxford University Press, London and New York 1964

Awooner-Renner, Bankole, *West African Soviet Union*, Wans Press, London 1946

Barnes, Leonard, *Soviet Light on the Colonies*, Penguin, London 1944

Boersner, Demetrios, *The Bolsheviks and the National and Colonial Question (1917–28)*, Droz, Geneva 1957

Brockway, Fenner, *Inside the Left*, Allen & Unwin, London 1942; New Leader, London 1942, 1947

Bibliography

Broderick, Francis, *W. E. B. DuBois*, Stanford University Press, Stanford 1959

Campbell, Alexander, *Empire in Africa*, Left Book Club, London 1944

Chattopadhyaye, V., "Report on the First International Conference of Negro Workers", *Daily Worker*, August 7, 1930

"Civil Liberty and the Colonies", prepared by the Overseas Subcommittee of the National Council on Civil Liberties, London, April 1945

Coser, Lewis, and Howe, Irving, *The American Communist Party*, Beacon Press, Boston 1957

Cronon, Edmund, *Black Moses*, University of Wisconsin Press, Madison 1962

Cudjoe, S. D., *Aids to African Autonomy*, College Press, London, July 1949, reprinted May 1950

Cunard, Nancy, *Negro Anthology*, Lawrence and Wishart, London 1934; ed., *Authors Take Sides*, Left Review Publications, London 1938

Davis, Helen, "Rise and Fall of George Padmore as a Revolutionary Worker", *Negro Worker*, August 1934

Decraene, Phillippe, *Le Pan Africanisme*, Presses Universitaires, Paris 1961

Donkor, Albert, *Soliloquy of Africa*, Accra n.d. (1960?)

Dover, Cedric, *Hell in the Sunshine*, Secker and Warburg, London 1943

Drake, St Clair, "Rise of the Pan-African Movement", *Africa Special Report*, Washington, April 1958

DuBois, W. E. B., *Dusk of Dawn*, Harcourt Brace, New York 1940; *In Battle for Peace*, Masses and Mainstream, New York 1952

"Europe's Difficulty is Africa's Opportunity", Manifesto of the International African Service Bureau, London, printed in *New Leader*, September 23, 1938

First International Trade Union Committee of Negro Workers: Resolutions, Hamburg 1930

"For a New Africa. Proceedings of the Conference on Africa, New York, April 14, 1944", New York 1944

Ford, James W., "MacDonald Prohibits ITUC-NW Meeting", *Pan-Pacific Monthly*, June–July 1930; "Report on the Geneva Conference", *International Press Correspondence* (*INPRECORR*), July 23, 1931 (later published as "Imperialism Destroys the People of Africa" in *Negro Problem* series, CPUSA, New York n.d.); "World Problems of Negro Peoples: A Refutation of George Padmore", CPUSA, New York 1934; and Gannes, Harry, "War in Africa", CPUSA, New York 1935; "Communists and the Struggle for World Liberation" (six of his African speeches), CPUSA, Harlem n.d.; et al., "Is Japan the Champion of the Colored Races?", CPUSA, New York, August 1938

Ghanaian Times, Padmore memorial issue, September 23, 1964

Gitlow, Benjamin, *I Confess*, Dutton, New York 1940

"Give Away the Colonies! Cranks—and a Few Others—in Conference", *East Africa* (later *East Africa and Rhodesia*), London, November 7, 1935

Hempstone, Smith, *The New Africa*, Faber, London 1961; re-titled

Africa—Angry Young Giant, Praeger, New York 1961; "Padmore and Pan-Africanism", *Report SH-144*, Institute of Current World Affairs, New York, March 2, 1959

Howe, Russell Warren, Padmore obituary in *Encounter*, December 1959

Hunton, Alphaeus, *Africa Fights for Freedom*, New Century, New York 1950; *Decision in Africa*, International Publishers, New York 1957

Italiaander, Rolf, *Schwarze Haut im Roten Griff*, Econ-Verlag, Düsseldorf 1962

James, C. L. R., "History of Negro Revolt", *Fact*, Special Issue, September 1938; *Mariners, Renegades and Castaways*, privately printed, New York 1953; *Black Jacobins*, 2nd ed. rev., privately printed, New York 1963

Jones-Quartey, K. A. B., *A Life of Azikiwe*, Penguin, Harmondsworth 1965

Kimble, David, *A Political History of Ghana*, Oxford University Press, London and New York 1963

Legum, Colin, *Must We Lose Africa?*, W. H. Allen, London 1954; "Bandung, Cairo and Accra. A Report on the First Conference of Independent African States", Africa Bureau, London 1958; *Pan-Africanism, A Short Political Guide* (rev. ed.), Pall Mall, London 1965; Praeger, New York 1965; "Socialism in Ghana", in Friedland, William, and Rosberg, Carl, eds., *African Socialism*, Hoover Institution, Stanford University Press, Stanford 1964; "Pan-Africanism or Communism", in Hamrell, Sven, and Widstrand, Carl, eds., *The Soviet Bloc, China and Africa*, Pall Mall, London 1964

Matchet's Diary, *West Africa*, October, 3 1959

McKenzie, Kermit, *The Comintern and World Revolution, 1928–43*, Columbia University Press, New York 1964

Munger, Edwin, "The All-African Peoples' Conference", *American Universities Field Staff Report*, New York, AUFS–ESM–1–1959; "Jimmy Markham", *Africa Special Report*, December 1958

Nelkin, Dorothy, "Socialist Sources of Pan-African Ideology", in Friedland and Rosberg, eds., *African Socialism*, Stanford University Press, Stanford 1964

"Nigerian Students' Voice", No. 1, New York, March 1964

Nkrumah, Kwame, *Ghana, the Autobiography of Kwame Nkrumah*, Nelson, New York 1957; *Towards Colonial Freedom*, Heinemann, London 1962; *Africa Must Unite*, Praeger, New York 1963; Heinemann, London 1963

Nolan, William, *Communism and the Negro*, Regnery, Chicago 1951

Oak, Vishnu Vitthal, *The Negro Newspaper*, Antioch Press, Yellow Springs, Ohio 1948

Ottley, Roi, *New World A-Coming*, Houghton Mifflin, Boston 1943; *No Green Pastures*, Scribner, New York 1951

Padley, Walter, "Empire or Free Union?", *Politics*, Spring 1948

Phillips, John, *Kwame Nkrumah and the Future of Africa*, Praeger, New York 1961; Faber, London 1961

Bibliography

Program of the American Negro Labor Congress, New York *c.* 1926

Raymond, Robert, *Black Star in the Wind*, MacGibbon and Kee, London 1960

Report of the Fourth Congress of the Red International of Labour Unions, London, July 1928

"Resolutions Adopted by the ITUC-NW at Hamburg", *INPRECORR*, June 2, 1931

Resolutions and Official Proceedings of the National Negro Congress, Chicago, February 14–16, 1936

Reynolds, Reginald, *My Life and Crimes*, Jarrolds, London 1956

Rogers, Joel A., *World's Great Men of Color*, privately printed, New York 1947

Rohdie, Samuel, "The Gold Coast Aborigines Abroad", *Journal of African History*, Vol. VI, No. 3, 1965

State Training School: Reading Material on the Negro Question, New York *c.* 1931

"Statement of the International Control Commission", *Negro Worker*, June 1934

The Atlantic Charter and Africa from an American Standpoint, Committee on Africa, the War and Peace Aims, New York 1942

The Communist Conspiracy. Strategy and Tactics of World Communism. Part I, Sections C and D. World Congresses, House of Representatives Committee on Un-American Activities, Washington 1956

Timothy, Bankole, *Kwame Nkrumah: His Rise to Power*, Allen & Unwin, London 1955

Valtin, Jan (Richard Krebs), *Out of the Night*, Heinemann, London 1941

Wilson, William, "Report on the Hamburg Conference", *Pan-Pacific Monthly*, September–October 1930

Yergan, Max, *Gold and Poverty in South Africa*, International Industrial Relations Institute, The Hague and New York 1938

PRIVATE PAPERS

I am indebted to:

Dr Herbert Aptheker, literary executor of W. E. B. DuBois, for examining the DuBois papers for Padmore content on my behalf;

Dennis Dobson, Padmore's London publisher, for allowing me to examine their correspondence;

Daniel Guerin, the noted French socialist, for sending me photo copies of his correspondence with Padmore;

Miss Iris Semper, Padmore's sister-in-law, and Dudley Cobham, Padmore's friend, for allowing me to quote from and use certain letters and photos in their possession;

Charles Lahr, for allowing me access to his complete file of the *New Leader* and the *Tribune*;

Mr Y. Berger of Tel Aviv, for his Comintern memoirs.

Index

Index

Index

Index

Macmillan, William, 44–5
McNair, John, 52, 56–7, 59, 72, 97–8, 108
Madagascar, 113, 123
Makonnen, T. Ras, 42, 83–4, 87, 91, 104n., 110, 133
Malvern, Lord, 45
Manchester Congress, 84, 86, 91, 94–100, 103, 106
Mannin, Ethel, 43
Manuilsky, Dmitri Zakarevich, 14, 16
Mao Tse-tung, 15
Maran, René, 81
Markham, James, 133
Marx, Karl, 86, 88
Mau Mau, 122n.
Mbadiwe, K. O., 82
Mendelson, Saul, 101
Menon, Krishna, 47
Michelet, Raymond, 30, 84
Miller, Kelly, 21–2
Milliard, Peter M., 83, 87, 89, 91, 94
Monnerot, Jules, 37
Moody, Dr Harold, 40n., 41–2, 59, 82–3, 88–9, 106
Moon, Thomas Parker, 71
Moore, Richard B., 8, 24
Moral Rearmament, 130
Morris, Sampson, 88, 92, 132
Moscow, 11, 12, 14–16, 20, 31, 37; *Daily News*, 15
Mossell, A. A., 88
Moton, Robert, 22
Movement for Colonial Freedom (MCF), 55, 113
Moyne, Lord, 54, 59; Report on West Indies, 67
Munger, Dr Edwin, 136–8
Münzenberg, Willi, 11
'Mussolini over Africa', 46

Narayan, Jayaprakesh, 78
Nashville, 4–5, 7
Nasser, President, 135

National Assoc. for Advancement of Coloured Peoples (NAACP), 13, 28–9, 41, 86, 90, 93–4, 97
National Assoc. of Socialist Students (NASSO), 133–5
National Council for Civil Liberties, 55
National Council for Nigeria and Cameroons (NCNC), 95, 106, 122
National Peace Council, 44
Negro Anthology, 27–30, 36, 61, 84
Negro Champion, 8
Negro in the Caribbean, The, 84
Negro Problem series, 25, 37
Negro Welfare Assoc. (NWA) 43, 54, 59
Negro Worker, 18–19, 21, 24–5, 28, 30, 32, 34, 51
Negro Workers and the Imperialist War, 22n., 24
Negro World Unity Congress, 39
Nehru, Jawaharlal, 47
New African, 99
New Barnet: Federal Unionist meeting, 58
New Leader, 46, 49, 52–3, 66, 67n., 70, 98
New York, 6–9, 28, 67, 81–2
Nicholson, R., 45
Nigeria, 17, 18, 54n., 64, 82, 90, 106; Padmore and, 104, 112–14, 122, 127, 131–2; Nigerian Workers' Union, 51
Nikoi, G. Ashie, 97, 120
Nkrumah, Kwame, 58n., 81–2, 87, 88n., 109; association with Padmore, 91–2, 95–7, 114–15, 121, 130, 132–5, 137; *Autobiography*, 120; becomes secretary of WANS, 99–100, 106; Ghana action campaign begins, 107; Padmore's admiration for, 116–17, 119–20, 123, 131; tributes to Padmore, 139–40
No Green Pastures, 17n.
Nurse, Alphonso, 2
Nurse, James, 2, 88